THE
EVERYDAY
SHAMAN

THE EVERYDAY SHAMAN

One Man's Journey into the Miraculous

JEFFREY BRUNK

The Everyday Shaman
Copyright © 2017 Soulshine Press

All rights reserved. No part of this publication may be reproduced or transmitted in any form or by any means electronic or mechanical, including photocopy, recording, or any information storage and retrieval system now known or to be invented, without permission in writing from the author, except by a reviewer who wishes to quote brief passages in connection with a review written for inclusion in a magazine, newspaper, broadcast or online forum

Library of Congress Cataloging-in-Publication Data available.

ISBN: 978-0-9992926-0-0
Printed in the United States of America

Editorial development and creative design support by Ascent:
www.itsyourlifebethere.com

Follow Jeffrey:
JeffreyBrunkTheEverydayShaman FunkyBrunky @BrunkJeffrey
www.EverydayShaman.net // www.ReikiMasterJeff.com

Dedication and Thanks

I dedicate this to those who always believed in me, the ones who never doubted me, and the ones who refused to abandon me during the many times throughout my journey when they were most needed. Their enduring impact is immeasurable.

Those individuals are
my mom, Brenda Brunk;
dad, Gene Brunk;
sister, Kelly Brunk;
grandmother, Eusebia Moore Petree;
and my butterfly, Pamela Ann Brunk.

I also dedicate this to the brave people who have and will question themselves and their perceptions of life, and set off on personal journeys in search of self.

Last, but certainly not least,
I dedicate this to our home, planet Earth, and the sustenance and healing she continues to provide to humanity.

Peace,
Jeffrey Brunk,
The Everyday Shaman

CONTENTS

Prologue :: *Whoa, Did You Feel that Too?* 9

1 :: Bridges 15

2 :: Things Go Dark 25

3 :: Things Come Apart 45

4 :: The Show 59

5 :: Marching into a War Zone 77

6 :: No-Man's Land 91

7 :: The Chaos Zone 99

8 :: The Power 115

9 :: Eyes and Ears Open 127

10 :: Passion and Purpose 131

11 :: Well, That Was Different 147

12 :: Communion and Confirmation 167

Epilogue 175

Acknowledgements 181

About the Author 182

PROLOGUE

WHOA, DID YOU FEEL THAT TOO?

THIS IS NOT a paint by numbers, "how to" guide to self-awareness. Nor is it another rehashed, pleasant memoir detailing a smooth "spiritual awakening." If anything, it's more of a "what not to do" guide—a personal story with quite a few corkscrew twists and an unexpected outcome. The outcome is one that I don't consider being as much "spiritual awakening" as "divinely inspired upheaval."

More than that, though, it's tale that I offer to encourage you. Listen, when the voice of awakening arises in you. Regardless of the journey it takes you on, it's well worth what you'll discover.

That said, I'll preface my tale of upheaval and learning with a bit of insight that came as a direct result of the wild and amazing ride that follows.

Bear with me. Then, hang on tight.

We all have something in common—something very personal yet profoundly universal. We share this with everyone we've ever known, those we've never known, those who lived eons before we were born and those who've yet to be born. Within each of us is a common spark. An unseen light—a connection that ties us to things greater than we perceive with the normal senses. We naturally know the outer, visible world, and we've become damned good at adhering to the rules it instills in us.

The *something* I'm referring to is much more potent than the conscious, daytime, dressed-for-success, corporal people we know ourselves to be. This something—this spark of light—knows us intimately and better than we know ourselves. It constantly flickers, wanting to make itself known. Relentless, that spark of light will at some point in your life flare up, saying, "Do not ignore me." When that happens, it's up to each of us to decide whether we'll be burned by the light or let it illuminate and lead us on a path through the darkness.

With the many distractions in our day to day lives, why do we care? Yeah, we can all recall at least one time in which we received a message of insight, a surprise bolt of wisdom, a seemingly miraculous healing, an uncomfortable sense of warning, a sudden change of mind or a tugging that caused us to take a different direction. Some shrug it off or call it human instinct, but if that's all it is how does it possess so much innate wisdom and insight and sometimes even knowledge of events about to take place?

And why do some of us hear this call and feel its pull more strongly than others? Most times, we don't share these feelings and moments to others because when we do we're made to feel strange. Are we just anomalies then? Are we crazy?

No, not crazy at all. Though some would argue that is the case.

The fact is, *many* of us feel the pull to open ourselves to something that lies very deeply within us—something beyond what we can touch and see.

We are the ones who walk between the visible world and the world of invisible realities. We see the unseen, hear what others do not hear, and listen to the whispers that others ignore. We are the ones who connect with the natural and universal energies that empower and heal.

Yet, we're like anyone else. We go about our everyday lives—getting the oil changed in our cars, sitting at our kids' sporting or musical events, picking up dogfood and toilet paper at the grocery store, groaning over unexpected bills . . . you know, the mundane things and the necessary things that worldly life requires of us.

We are shamans in blue jeans, as it were. What I refer to as *everyday shamans*.

Shamanism, for me, was a word that conjured up the mental image of a witchdoctor, nose pierced with a chicken bone—a picture taken right out of an episode of "Gilligan's Island".

Uh, nope. I do not have a chicken-bone piercing. Yet.

On the contrary.

Shamanism isn't a religion. It is a way of life, one that has been practiced in one form or another by individuals in virtually every culture for millennia. Unlike its darker counterparts such as voodoo, shamanism is a well-intentioned practice used by men and women who have listened to the whispers, embraced that flickering spark and fanned it into a flame. Why? Because that spark of light within us beckons us to bring healing, betterment and enlightenment, as well as help others establish the connection to the true "Self" and this spinning, blue orb we inhabit.

A word of warning: Shamans occasionally practice with not-so-well-intentioned motives. There's this thing called Karma, however, and when Karma visits, it shows up at the door with ten pounds of shit *for every pound that the shaman doles out. That's another matter....*

Simply stated, our planetary home is sick. Commode-hugging sick. A rapidly changing climate, extreme weather, never-before-seen levels of pollution in the seas, skies and soil, the extinction of many species and near-extinction of others—humanity included—are glaring signs that our distressed planet is sweating out a fever. Humanity—patient zero—is suffering and sweating profusely in unison. As our planet changes, if humanity is to survive, something needs to drastically change. Mother Nature is pissed and humanity is seemingly indifferent.

Here is the ugly truth—that divine spark inside has slowly been engulfed in a glob of muck. Materialism, career, image, the pursuit of money and "stuff" and the multitude of distractions has slowly been stifling the inner whispers and dimming the inner flame. Those things only briefly satisfy a deeply felt need for something more, something we search for yet can't quite seem to find; the spark—the common thread inside—our connection to everyone and everything.

It is the authentic self that shows us our purpose and meaning. I must have had a past life with one hell of an "'It's all about me'" mindset, because Karma stretched out in the backseat and was an annoying backseat driver during my journey in search of both self and spiritual awareness. Fortunately, Karma seems to have both a Master's degree and a PhD in teaching. *Good thing... Karma would need it, to reach and teach me.* The story of how I was led along the path from materialism to the incredible world of shamanism is the subject of this book. It isn't necessarily a pretty story filled with unicorns, ponies and rainbows.

And yet the purpose of my writing is not to focus on myself and my experiences, but to show others that there is a path. In my case, I was a bit of a slow learner so the path was littered with potholes. Mistakes, delays, and detours came my way fast, furiously and frequently. There is no denying that others were hurt by some of my actions; I hurt myself. So, that is why I offer certain parts of my story as a cautionary tale of what not to do should you heed the call and embark on your own journey to discover your higher self and your true, spiritual purpose

The path I followed led me to places, sights and experiences I'd never have known existed had I not tuned out the static. Everyone travels a path that can lead to what shamanism offers. My advice? Choose wisely. Every choice leads to a destination—some good, others not so much.

A single spark, where connection to the whole occurs is what we all share. And a single spark—if you nurture it—is all that's needed to be an everyday shaman.

Now, get comfortable, grab some popcorn and your favorite beverage and let's take a little ride.

1

BRIDGES

*To start down a new and unknown path,
sometimes everything you know and everything
you're doing must stop making sense.*

JUST ANOTHER DAY IN PARADISE, I thought. It wasn't sarcasm, it was a way to put a positive spin on what had become a negative reality.

These words came to mind with increasing frequency, dominating my thoughts along with the vision of a paradise that Ebenezer Scrooge would find delightful. They began resonating with me as a direct reflection of the man I had become—a man who was once a boy looking at the world as his oyster but who had grown to be a model of conformity—an oyster on the half shell without a pearl . . . or melted butter.

It would be years before I saw the truth clearly: I had been molded gradually by the world I lived in, trained and expected to be a man who would bend and attend to the needs and wants of everyone—employers, wife, kids, friends, acquaintances, the government, the dog... everyone except myself—and I was playing the role very well. Playing the same role every single day, however, makes Jeff a dull boy. Especially when I'd started to sense I was living out a role I was born to play.

Just another freakin' day in freakin' paradise.
The words were a true expression of a normal guy lacking sense of meaning. Even deeper, a sense of identity. I didn't consciously realize at the time that another self was clobbering the door, two-fisted and furious, demanding to be recognized.

"If this is what it feels like to be in paradise, heaven must really suck," I muttered, as I walked upstairs to the master bedroom.

Nicely carpeted stairs—tan carpet, the most bland and neutral color that exists—were the first thing one noticed when entering the house. It was a nice house with a crappy front yard. But the house, oh, it shined inside. Despite two young children occupying the house with me and my wife there were no signs of disorder. The interior resembled a builder's model home—tastefully decorated without a hint of dust and nothing out of place. It was how my wife, a rising executive with a large property management company, wanted the house to look—that is, as it came out of a *House Beautiful* magazine.

Today, the fifteen steps from the foyer to the upstairs level felt like the Long Mile in a prison. My thoughts were jumbled and relentless. Lately, the type of person I really was, wanted, and needed to be, clashed in every way with who I had let myself become. Hell, by participating in the life everyone else wanted me to live *I* was assaulting *myself.*

But who was that?

Sure, I could have blamed it on giving in to others' demands and expectations. I had grown up at a time when societal, parental and educational expectations were firmly defined—one graduates from high school and goes to college, graduates from college and finds a job, achieves a level of success that assures meeting and marrying the "one", and later starts a family (two children, one of each sex; the ideal).

I wasn't into blaming anyone, though. *I chose this life. I shouldn't have these feelings*, I thought. I had no right to feel unhappy, did I? Okay, so I'd tried like hell to throw a knockout punch to the small whispers that had plagued me since childhood, but I'd always caved-in to expectations. After all, it was selfish to think of myself first, wasn't it? I had a duty to do well for the sake of good people who'd raised me to work hard and be responsible. And I'd done my damnedest to live up to their hopes for me.

C'mon, face it Jeff . . . you have always been a pleaser.

I reached the top of the stairs and stopped. *I reached everyone else's goals. Yeah, so what? And* now *what?*

I shook my head. I didn't have time for whatever silly midlife crisis was trying to hatch. I needed to get things done. Like everyone else I knew, there was a full day's agenda to be met—normal errands to be run, normal deadlines to be met.

Normal—a synonym for boring.

Still, the feeling persisted that something needed to change, and was about to.

The first order of business was dropping off my children to daycare. After a quick, "I love you," and "Have fun!" my son and daughter hopped from the back seat and headed for the entrance. I smiled and nodded towards Ms. Kathy, then pulled away and began the five-minute drive back to our neighborhood. The feeling was even stronger now, that for me today was *not* normal and this all this was *not my life.*

I turned left onto our steeply sloped driveway and eased the Toyota Camry into the garage. The last several years I'd driven a Mazda MPV, which I'd jokingly dubbed the "Silver Bullet," in a light-hearted attempt to save a bit of male dignity. The Camry wasn't the '67 Corvette I'd dreamt of owning since my teenage years, but it didn't scream "Domesticated!" quite as loudly as the minivan had.

Domesticated—the synonym for tamed. More about being a domesticated human creature later. A lot more . . . .

My wife had been leaving the house much earlier each morning, eager to get to work. Her new position within the organization demanded much more of her time and attention. As a result, her life's ease and comfort required much more of my time and attention. The day to day management of my wife's and family's needs was now overshadowing the importance of my work as an art director and as a freelancer.

Is that it, I thought. *Am I just irritated because her career is running the show?* Is that why I feel off-kilter? Then I smiled, realizing that was how many women must feel, living in the shadow of their husband's career demands.

But . . . no, I could honestly say that wasn't it. On the other hand, I had become concerned that money was becoming everything.

Back inside, I headed up to the bedroom again, to shower, dress, and start my own day. The walk upstairs was noticeably different this morning. It seemed like I wasn't hyper-alert for some reason. Everything felt off or disjointed. Glancing up, the hand-painted decorative plates mounted on the wall above the stairwell suddenly seemed like signs or portents. On one level, I'd had no input in choosing them. But on another level, they represented a strong impression of the bigger picture that was slowly coming into focus.

This. Is. Not. Your. Life. I'm like an animal that followed the scent of bait down the wrong path, and wound up caught in a trap.

Where did that come from?

Walking down the carpeted hallway of the second floor, I stopped and looked directly into the master bedroom.

"*Master*, huh?" I asked myself. "Master of *what*?"

As I walked into the bedroom, my thoughts ran over the events of the morning. Wake up, feed the kids, tell the wife to have a good day, drop the kids at daycare—*check*. Now, work on that freelance project . . . .

With a quick glance from the bedroom window, I noticed something interesting about the house sitting opposite ours: It was nearly identical to ours.

Damn, it was nearly identical to every house in the neighborhood.

The paint color was different and the lawn was better manicured, but otherwise our houses were remarkably similar, and for the first time I realized the significance of this.

Cue the genuinely significant thought.

I was about to turn away when out of nowhere . . .

What if under the surface we are more than these conformed people, all pressed into a mold? What if there's a lot more to every one of us than meets the eye?

I shook my head. Where was *this* coming from?

And then something much more profound occurred.

A persistent restlessness I'd been troubled by for years became a strong sense that something was truly "off"—not bad, just off.

Open your eyes. Look around. What do you see?

I stared at the details in the homes. While I took in the similarities of each home, I saw everything with super intensity.

You feel *like you're in a trap, because you* are.

At that moment, I seemed to feel something that can only be called a vibration.

Still staring out at the neighbor's houses, I had the very strong impression that the houses were not real. No, that wasn't exactly it. Of course, the houses were real, as in, solid, but they and everything else—the lawns, the cars, the street—all of it was just a curtain, and behind it all lay something else.

Okay, that was too strange. I wanted to shake off this sensation. The thing was, I couldn't.

I looked again, and it was as if my vision had changed. Things looked different.

Outside, the day was still sunny—yet the vibrant shades of the natural world went dim. No brilliance or color radiated from anything. Strange, since it was a late summer day, with beautiful sunny skies and no clouds in the crystal blue air.

At that moment, from the surrounding houses, an almost choreographed opening of garage doors occurred—followed by an exodus of neighbors in cars, each one perfectly corresponding with the rung of the corporate ladder that each driver had climbed. There went the lower level managers, followed closely by the high level ones—supervisors . . . .

Acutely aware, I observed it all in detail—not with judgment or criticism, but with flash after flash of insight.

- » *We are so focused on the material world.*
- » *We don't see what's important.*
- » *We're focused on the distractions.*
- » *We are more than our possessions and positions.*
- » *We have deeper identities than we can possibly imagine....*

I shook my head. *What the hell?* What was this shift taking place, and why was the outer world dimming, while—what could I call it? the truth? the reality that lay behind physical things?—was becoming so clear.

Since this event was nothing I'd sought or asked for, it was unsettling.

Enough of being a "garage voyeur," I thought, pulling myself away from the window. The freelance project awaited.

I went to the kitchen to grab some juice from the fridge and, try as I might to dive into my "normal" day, the unusual experience followed me. I was not ready to recognize much less deal with something as profound as some reality that lay beyond this one There was work to be done, money to be made, sheets to be pressed....

Dear Lord, I'm pressing sheets. What the hell is wrong with me?

That prompted me to go through the very solid, in-this-world reasons why I was feeling detached from my life.

First, there was the life path my wife and I were on.

Every morning for several years, I had proudly witnessed my wife go off to her burgeoning successful career, which caused us to thrive financially. I had played a role in her successes by vigorously supporting her efforts. She had stepped up the first rung, then the second, the third and was headed, we were sure, for the top. She was just *amazing* at her work.

Yet, with each step up that ladder, I now admitted, I'd found myself further below, watching. Was that it? Why I feel like I was not just out-of-sync with a job or a career track, but also somehow way out of focus at a deep level? Did I need to make more progress on my own career path as an art director, maybe climb a corporate ladder myself?

Unexpected as a clap of thunder out of a clear summer sky another impression came—
NO.
—and with it another faint sense of vibration.
I paused, glass of orange juice halfway to my lips. *Where is this coming from? This is just weird*, I thought. *I'm losing it.*
Then came another lightning-strong and clear thought.
Who are *you, and what are you* doing*?*
I'd later realize it was strange that I didn't freak out or question a voice in my head that was not my own. At that moment, it didn't strike me as odd or make me distrust my sanity. I had the conviction that I needed to focus on the question itself.
That urge did not last long, however. I couldn't just stop and go into an impromptu, profound soul search for *the real me* and my *own personal life path.* The to-do list was still shouting at me.

Enough, I thought. *Next thing you know you'll be having out of the body experiences. Negatory on that, good buddy.*

If I'd known then what I know now about all that lay ahead from that point, I would probably have run away screaming . . . but then I'd have missed the adventure of a lifetime.
I had no way of knowing that what I'd experienced as strange vibrations was actually a kind of bridge, a deeper way of knowing,

that can cause those who sense them to connect from the mundane, visible world to other and greater realities of the unseen. And what I'd touched that morning turned out to be the first tiny step on a long journey.

I now know that some of us reach a point in life where we are unsettled simply because we're in the wrong line of work. In that case, a career change is in order. But for some of us, the unsettledness is a signpost, pointing to an entirely different path we're meant to follow—one that has nothing at all to do with outer world careers, material success, or even the visible, physical world itself. Some—maybe many more of us than are willing to admit it—are called to a journey into realms that lie all around us, invisible to the naked eye. And though other people will say we are insane to even speak of such things as if they're real, *we know they are*. And so most of us are left to make the journey there and back largely on our own.

This is my story about my journey. I tell it so that you who know what I'm talking about may avoid the missteps I made and the things I allowed to happen to me, and so that you will not have to go it alone.

2

THINGS GO DARK

WHEN A LIGHT COMES ON inside you, it may not be a glaring beam of light but more of a nightlight.

That's because the first thing it may show you is how devoid of true vitality and meaning things are.

(Did I mention, I have an inner narrator? Sometimes he's insightful, much of the time he's a wise ass. Just a warning.)

Two houses down from ours in the *cul-de-sac* on which we lived was the dead-end circle.

The day after I'd looked out a window and seen our neighborhood differently, I woke and saw my whole life in a different light. Not a pleasant one.

I was still focused primarily on the outer circumstances of my life. In the aftermath of yesterday's strange "sensings", I found myself still thinking of it as an empty shell.

It was true that my wife was well on her way to becoming a great success, and I was proud of her achievements. But this morning, another impression arose.

You're not a husband. You're not a partner.

Again—where was that coming from? It was true that something had not been right with our marriage for some time, at least in my eyes. *I was an employee,* someone hired and managed by someone else in order to create a partnership for the betterment of all involved. I was most definitely enjoying the fruits of my wife's success, or at least I had been. Though we had started out in with next to nothing—as many newlyweds do—in that moment, the material gains ceased to be of importance to me, and my unclear sense of who I was and who I was meant to be superseded all the "employment benefits" of our lifestyle.

Yeah, but they were nice benefits. Oh wait, they were bait, the cheese in the mousetrap—right?

Stepping outside to retrieve the morning paper, I looked at the houses and the *cul-de-sac*. The symbolism all around me smacked me in the head like a middle-school bully.

Not only am I an employee, I live on a freakin' dead-end street. Talk about symbolism. On top of that, I'm surrounded by people who don't seem to know there is more to this world than what we can own or see.

Okay, this was not about other people. I sensed that. Whatever was going on inside was about me. This world, nice at it was, was not one where *I* necessarily belonged.

That felt odd.

Then oddly freeing.

Then again, I'd never really felt as if this world was where I belonged.

For several moments, I experienced a crystal clarity that this sense of being wide awake and outside of time was the right place to be. Along with that, I felt the deep conviction that I needed to be doing something different with my life.

But I was on *this* road, having arrived here because I'd chosen to make a left instead of a right turn. I'd not followed the yearning to go to New York, with art school degree in hand after graduation or move across the country, float around in Santa Monica and live the beach bum lifestyle.

Yeah, but think of what you'd have missed if you'd taken that right turn.

With that I dropped back into the sense of being trapped in a life that was not mine. And *that* thought—that I was "trapped" in my life—came with a huge side-serving of raw guilt. After all, I had a nice house, a wife, two healthy children, nice clothes, two new cars. I had a job, one of many, that was okay most of the time.

Still, the sense of detachment from the world I was living in was real. So was the sense of being alone—not as in alone in an empty house, but alone in a packed house and world of people grabbing for all the goodies we could grab. Maybe the aloneness was why my inner narrator had emerged—like a crazy, often joking, *goomba* to keep myself company.

Despite the occasional raised eyebrow and eyeroll from others, it's been good for me. Was it good for you?

Just now the humorous voice of "Jeff" wasn't helping.

I felt empty and in search of purpose. The irony of living on a literal dead-end street was both sickening and chuckle-worthy. I had accepted the role of "employee." And as I thought about it, not only had I conformed my life to hers—no fault on her part, certainly—I'd conformed to society's examples and expectations of how to be a husband, father, church member, neighbor, and friend.

As usual, I tried to get myself to see the dark humor here.

C'mon, Jeff. You got yourself into this. Conformity is a form of surrender and it was nobody's fault but yours.

In a way that was true. Separating me from the person I was meant to be, whoever that was, had come about through a whole lifetime of choices *I* had made—to please my family, friends, fellow church members, bosses on my career track and even the dog.

That's all, I thought bitterly. *Just a whole freakin' lifetime of choices I made for other people.*

How was I supposed to undo or change that?

I went through my routine most of that day like a man in a waking trance. I tried to make sense of what *I* had done, which was this:

I had made my way into the wrong life—and now I was also feeling both a huge load of guilt that I didn't fully appreciate what I had, and a second load of regret that I was way off the mark from something that those strong impressions were telling me I needed to be doing instead.

Enough, enough, enough.

I felt as if I should just shut down this whole inner trip I was on right now. If I made any big change, I thought, it would bring my whole life crashing down around me and several other people, and that was unacceptable.

I retreated into denial. I would just avoid these weird sensations, these "vibes" and these tangled thoughts, and all of it would go away. I'd keep freelancing, and we'd keep buying more cool stuff.

Yeah, that was a good plan. That really worked well, didn't it Jeff?

Late that afternoon, I retrieved the kids from daycare and was dutifully preparing dinner while the music of Jimmy Buffett echoed throughout the house. I felt relieved from this morning's torments, because music was, and had always been, a great equalizer for me.

Time to mention the soundtrack, Jeff.

I'd always maintained that my life had its own soundtrack, and many of my life's significant moments were linked in some manner to a specific song or lyric. Jimmy Buffett's music had always spoken to the part of me that is full of awe and in search of adventure, wanderlust, beauty and freedom. For many years, his songs provided me with confidence and reassurance.

While I chopped and minced onion, parsley and garlic, preparing yet another gourmet dinner, as was another duty I'd assumed, the Buffett tune, "Growing Older, But Not Up" began to play. I had listened to this song countless times over the years. This time I was struck by one particularly foretelling lyric:

> *I'm growing older, but not up.*
> *My metabolic rate is pleasantly stuck.*
> *So let the winds of change blow over my head.*
> *I'd rather die while I'm living, than live while I'm dead.*

As if I was hearing it for the very first time, those last two lines of the lyric stabbed me in the heart. The last line especially stuck like a dart in a bull's-eye. I repeated it to myself.

I'd rather die while I'm living, than live while I'm dead.

I didn't think at that moment that there are no coincidences. I only knew the timing was pleasantly eerie. The fact that those lyrics jumped out at me, despite having sung along to them dozens of times without a second thought, secured the song's place in my life's soundtrack album.

I put down the paring knife and looked in on my kids, who were playing in the family room. Seeing them made me smile. *What beautiful kids.* Inwardly, though, the lyrics kept repeating and causing more stabs of deep pain.

How do I live before I die? What does that mean for me? How do I find, much less get to that *life, when I'm here in* this *life?*

And then I thought, *I don't know the answers, but, one way or another, I have to do something to figure it all out. I have to.*

David R. Hawkins, internationally renowned physicist and spiritual teacher, says in his book, *Letting Go: The Pathway of Surrender,* "The person who suffers from inner poverty is relentlessly driven to accumulate on the material level."

Something inside me was waking up to the need for riches that lay beyond this material world.

That summer day, I was oblivious to having made a huge, life-altering decision: I handed in my notice, and unwittingly decided to go into business *for* myself, *as* myself.

Once I made this decision, though, I felt stuck in between two lives or two worlds. It was like leaving one room, expecting to step directly into another—only that didn't happen. I felt lost, and ironically, the first step in my new direction was down. In fact, stuck between two worlds is exactly what I was—or at least I was about to be.

"Depression"—what a great catch-all word—is what got me dragged to the office of my wife's doctor.

Come on. You got in the car of your own free will. You "went along to get along," like you always did.

The doctor ran a regular, run-of-the-mill practice, and my wife had been referred to him by one of her new coworkers soon after we had moved to Raleigh, North Carolina. The medical office was across town in a tidy medical park, and we arrived on-time for my appointment and easily found a place to park the car.

That would be the only easy thing about this visit.

I sauntered reluctantly towards the building, trailing after my wife by ten feet or more. Once inside, we scanned the building directory. Something deep inside asked, *What are you doing here?*—something that wanted to resist, turn around and run.

At that point, there wasn't enough of *me* yet, though, to help with the resistance effort.

Man the battle stations? Um, no. You just stood there like a deer in the headlights, letting someone else drag you through the motions because you didn't know what else to do.

As we entered the office building the thought occurred—really, though, what *was* I doing here? Why had my vital energies and sense of connection to something greater drained away so quickly?

Whenever there had been less than ideal circumstances in my life, I'd always taken the gut-punch, stood tall, and "sucked it up" with a wink and a smile. In fact, that was how I was raised, finding the humor in any tough experience. I'd coped with everything from the death of a loved one to being teased by the 'cool' kids at school about my weight. Humor helped to ensure my survival in this world, while I kept reaching for—what was it?

The sense of frustration weighed me down. So, in that sense, I suppose—though I hated to admit it—I was depressed.

Depressed, repressed, stressed, oppressed. Come on, Jeff, you felt all those things.

Others had noticed subtle changes. My parents and sister were seeing me far less often than they liked. The short, two-hour drive to visit them was now infrequent. And when we got together, my family was keenly aware of the changes in my demeanor. I wasn't the same outgoing, fun-loving, and resilient son and brother that they'd always known.

My wife had also been taking notes. She had been seeing small changes in the man she'd married, changes that provided excuses for nagging. She didn't understand what was happening, and she was understandably concerned. She'd married me with the knowledge that I was the living, breathing epitome of the one who inspired the phrase, "throwing caution to the wind." I was no longer that man.

Now, adding to my personal stress—and most definitely putting a crimp in our relationship—she bristled at the notion that she was now married to the man who personified "caution." I didn't throw it into the wind anymore. Nor could she understand why I no longer provided pithy comments or asked questions as she spoke of her travails and victories at work.

Okay, so I wasn't the life of the party, and maybe I was sullen and restless—discontent with a side order of sadness—but I didn't need to see a doctor just because I was no longer the way everyone else needed me to be.

So, what was I doing here?

The answer was simple. I was going along to get along. But

why? Because my wife and everyone else wanted me to be "normal" again?

And you didn't know what was "normal" for you, because you hadn't experienced it yet. That *was the problem.*

As the elevator rose to the third-floor doctor's suite, I recognized the Muzak version of "Tainted Love", the 1980s Soft Cell classic.

"Catchy," I remarked.

No response from my wife.

C'mon, not even a smile?

I could tell she was "in the zone", which was the business world. She'd been in it since we'd left the house. I felt as distant from her as she apparently felt from me.

When the elevator doors opened, I was surprised to be staring directly at the receptionist. She smiled as if we were old friends, and greeted us with a very southern drawl.

"Hey, how're y'all today?"

As we approached the beautiful and impressively large oak desk, I thought, *Someone around here is obviously compensating for something.*

Checked-in and unsure what to expect next, we looked around for two empty chairs in the waiting area. We chose our seats, partially based upon what magazines were on the adjacent, glass-top table. I dropped myself into the chair beside her and wasted no time in snatching a *Golf* magazine from a neat stack of periodicals. By all measures, this was a waiting room set up to make a certain, nice-level-of-income, upper-middle-class-lifestyle client feel welcome. Of course, I'd been in offices like this before—but today I felt like an alien here. Something really was not right, and I didn't think it was me.

When we were called into the examining room, several things jumped out at me right away. The first was that the 'doctor' who was there to examine me wasn't formally a doctor—she was a physician's assistant. She was in her early thirties, I guessed, and wore a white lab coat with an engraved name tag. She had her own office space which boasted a single window overlooking the busy street below and the surrounding buildings within the medical park complex. An office with a window is a big deal in the working world; this was enough for me to blindly accept with confidence that she knew what she was doing.

Big mistake.

To the right of the window, I noticed one thick book with three large, gold letters above the title on the spine. The DSM, the *Diagnostic and Standard Manual* used by shrinks to categorize disorders and illnesses, was on the bottom shelf propped beside a model of the human brain. I was certain that there would be a short synopsis at the end of the "Depression" chapter in the DSM that would eliminate me as a candidate for that diagnosis. I was unhappy and discontent for reasons that I didn't yet fully understand. That was dawning on me. But I was not depressed.

Fortunately, there was no examination table in the "examination" room, and I immediately felt a wave of relief.

At least they didn't require you to drop your pants, turn your head, and cough.

Years later I would think back to this omission of the usual medical protocol and slap myself across the back of the head. Warning signs were jumping out and trying to grab my attention. They were standing directly before me, yet I didn't see them. Nor did I listen to the inner voice that had become louder. It was saying,

Run.
Not used to obeying that inner awareness just yet . . . I stayed.

You should have run. Just sayin'. But no . . . .

My wife explained that I needed to be 'checked out,' since I'd not been my usual chipper self. I'd become more outspoken, more focused on myself than I'd been at any time in the previous years of our marriage. A description of the evolving me included the obvious.

I was simply no longer putting the wants of others at the top of my list, as I always had. My duty to adhere to the godly qualities of marital and familial selflessness was eroding.

It would be a long time before I recognized that an inner call to a new way to be can also be leading you away from an old, outmoded way that you once were. Right now, a new sense of needing to rebel against my old ways of being was starting to wreak a bit of havoc.

The truth was that *my wife* was uncomfortable with the person I was becoming, and I wasn't much help because I was not sure who that was.

"He's just not at all himself. He's like a stranger."

Allow me to provide an explanation.

In fact, the changes I was undergoing were ignited by rapidly growing frustrations, doubts, and uncertainties which, I was just beginning to realize, I had actually carried within me for years. My wife could see only outward expressions of what I felt as I'd begun to re-examine—well, pretty much everything. I felt, on the one hand, frustrated and angry, which was pulling me down, and on the other hand, I felt moments of elation, as if I were standing on the front edge of the world on an early morning, watching a new day about to be born.

The main problem was that I couldn't talk about these wildly swinging moods, brought on by the fact that a big shift was occurring inside me. An awakening, in its earliest stages. The fact was, if I voiced my questions and thoughts, it often led to heated exchanges and conflicts between us.

This was especially true when the subject involved church.

To suggest, for example, that Jesus might not be the *only* way to heaven or salvation or eternal bliss was considered as "sacrilege." Being "sentenced" by her as a heretic brought on bouts of guilt, anger, uncertainty, and resentment.

Later I'd wonder—why was questioning and honest seeking such a threat?

Even while living in the midst of all this, I must say, I had a subtle sense that positive changes, not negative ones, were going on within me—in fact, forcing themselves on me. But at this point that sense was usually overwhelmed by doubt. Though the recurrence of that "uncertain surety" was rare, and I had no clue what changes were occurring, I had fleeting moments when I felt something purely wonderful. A state of inner *peace*, like I was about to emerge from some great darkness and step out into light.

In a way, I was becoming like a stranger to myself, as the new awareness I'd been experiencing changed my perspective on life.

Before I had much of a chance to explain how I thought I was doing, my wife pointed a finger directly at my face and insisted, "You're not yourself anymore"—by which she meant, the guy who'd carried her off the dance floor over my shoulder on the night we first met.

Okay, so a rousing version of "Danger Zone" can cause me to act out, for sure, I thought. *Don't get me started on "Shout" from "Animal House." No one can "gator" like me.*

Before I could respond, she reported that she was not alone in her assessment of me. Pretty much her whole family, including her constantly-inebriated uncle, agreed after hearing of my 'symptoms' that I was "seriously depressed" and in need of medical attention if *our* lives were to ever be normal again.

There's that word again, "normal."

I sat in the consulting room as the physician's assistant eyed me, and thought, *"Normal" means being totally tamed and domesticated, and accepting that my life is complete, fulfilled mentally, professionally and spiritually.*

But it wasn't. Not at all. And what was I supposed to do with the wild, untamed energy I'd begun to feel churning down deep?

After a brief round of small-talk with me now—the weather, the kids, yada, yada, yada—the P.A. launched into a series of questions.

"Do you feel suicidal?"

"No."

Not quite true. I'd realized that the part of me that was awakening had in fact felt *dead* for some time, and really wanted *out*—whatever I needed to do to get there.

"Have you lost interest in things that once made you happy?"

My thoughts screamed, *Well, yes, but I'm not happy for reasons that would not sit well with others in this small room. Like climbing the success ladder, living like everyone else in our cloned community, going through the motions at church and everywhere else.*

My spoken answer, however, was an honest and understated "Yes."

I glanced around the office before resting my eyes on my wife's still smiling face. In an instant, one of those old, *Hey, I wonder if I can get 'perky' drugs out of this awkward situation?* thoughts popped into my mind. I didn't know of any 'perky' prescription drugs. My only reference was the cocaine, Everclear, and Dr. Pepper cocktails of many years before. I still occasionally found myself fondly reminiscing about the 1980s and the three years of those ten that I vaguely remembered. Those days were long gone, though. I'd survived, experienced much, loved many, and had no regrets. On the soul side of the ledger, thanks to a religious upbringing, I had no doubt that the cost for those days of fun and frivolity included a first-class seat on the red-eye flight to Hell. Years of hellfire and damnation sermons, Sunday school lessons, and self-inflicted Bible study reminded me of my potential fate if I strayed.

"Are you on any medications?"

I had never needed any type of daily medication for any sort of legitimate physical or mental ailment. On this day, though, that badge of honor was stripped from my Lifetime Achievements sash.

"No. Not taking anything."

The P.A. nodded, and scratched a final note on my file.

Her evaluation had concluded, and the aspiring doctor stepped out of the room leaving us alone to reflect on what had just happened. I was trying to make sense of what the hell was going on and how I'd allowed myself to even get here. I felt as if I had just been judged and deemed worthy to be involuntarily committed.

My wife and the P.A. had both nodded and offered understanding smiles. How could they understand what I did not? They seemed to believe they did. And their smiles were unnerving.

I suddenly realized my wife would have a medical professional's 'diagnosis' and a reason to believe that I had a foot planted on the road to the 'normalcy' she expected of me. As for me, I was afraid I'd get a diagnosis of 'crazy' based upon a few generic questions posed by a doctor who wasn't a doctor. Of course, the diagnosis would be served with another smile.

The examiner returned to the tiny room after a few short minutes. I imagined she'd probably gone to the receptionist's desk to chat about shoes or politics, allowing us to wait for her return while believing she was discussing my case with Johns Hopkins or the Mayo Clinic.

In her right hand, she held a pen and prescription pad. In her left, she clutched a small box. She sat down, and looked squarely at my wife as she began offering her professional diagnosis.

It was as if I were invisible. *If only . . .*

"In my opinion," she began, "after contemplating Jeff's responses, and your concerns about his behavior in addition to what I've myself noticed –"

Wait, hold the phone. What did she notice, and why wasn't she telling us, or at least me, the notice-ee?

—"leaves me with little doubt that he is suffering from clinical depression and quite possibly Bipolar Disorder."

Say what? Run that by me again.

Only then did she—and for only a moment—glance *my* way. Then, she quickly looked back towards and mainly spoke to my wife for the rest of her diagnostic explanation.

This is nothing more than this woman's opinion, I fumed. *We're not going to take this seriously. Remember what they say about people and opinions.*

"Hey, that's just... like, you know... your opinion, man."—The Dude (The Big Lebowski)

The medical establishment then had much more relaxed criteria in the determination of a diagnosis of a 'mental disorder.' That and, as I would later learn, the symptoms of depression and bipolar disorder can mirror those of one undergoing a spiritual awakening.

My wife's smile had brightened. She genuinely *smiled* as she took in the diagnosis.

When I saw that she was smiling, my face flashed what I was thinking, which was, *You've gotta be fuckin' kiddin' me.*

This woman I'd married appeared to be very happy to hear that I supposedly had a mental illness, while I had never heard the words 'Bipolar Disorder' in my life—and I was fairly certain neither had she.

I relayed that fact to the P.A. in the form of a stupid question. "Uh, what is Bipolar Disorder, and how did I get it?" Of course, my question was asked half in jest, I knew it wasn't contagious.

"Okay, in a nutshell, Bipolar Disorder is a mental condition that can cause mild or severe mood swings, depression, and even elation. Until recently, someone with Bipolar Disorder was known as being Manic-Depressive."

That was it. A sketchy synopsis at best—which too quickly morphed into directions on the proper way to take the life-changing medication gripped firmly in her left hand. I'm no doctor but I'm almost certain that any medical reference materials contain a more thorough explanation of Bipolar Disorder in the epilogue.

Displaying the little box holding all that was needed for me to reclaim myself, she said, "This is Wellbutrin, an antidepressant. This is only a sample to get you started, but I'm giving you a prescription that you're to take daily, in the morning, for the next thirty days. This should help you manage the ups and downs we're seeing. After thirty days, we'll see how you're doing."

The ups and downs that *we're* seeing? When did she first notice my ups and downs? I couldn't recall ever having her to the house for a visit.

And while I was at it—*what ups and downs? Manic-Depressive? Bipolar? Really?*

The overblown 'diagnosis' made about as much sense as digging a hole ten feet deep to plant a daisy. Beyond that, I didn't know what to think, other than, *Will these pills make me happy again?*

Okay, so there was something going on inside me. But it wasn't ups and downs. Some moments I experienced jubilation at an increasing self-awareness and at other times there was doubt and a nagging fear of change that I couldn't understand.

"How is this going to make me feel?" I asked.

"It will take three to four weeks before you start noticing any difference," the P.A answered. "Then, you should feel more 'even', more at ease and less anxious. You should feel happier and enjoy those things that you used to enjoy."

Basically, I'd just listened to a TV advertisement for Wellbutrin.

"Cool," I said. "Will it make me perky? You know—more *alive?*"

"Perky? I guess so," replied Dr. P.A. "Happier and more 'engaged' might be a better way to put it."

"Perky, happy, engaged, normal—however you choose to say it—works for me," my wife responded. "I just want him back to his old self. If this will make that happen, then we're all-in."

"We're all-in"?

As if she was also going to be partaking in the effects of this magical pill. My 'mental illness' wasn't contagious, but it surely felt as if it was. If only my wife had a crystal ball at that moment. Being 'all in' were words that would one day haunt her.

I just had to ask, half-joking. "Does this mean I'm crazy?"

"No! Not at all. But if you start feeling that you're becoming more depressed or begin to have any weird ideas or feel suicidal, call me."

Again, it sounded like another Wellbutrin ad—this time alluding to even more severe side-effects.

There was something in her response that undermined my confidence, my belief that I was not really suffering from a mental illness. It was the words, ". . . if you begin to have any weird ideas."

I'd been besieged by so-called weird ideas my entire life, just not the type of weird ideas that the P.A. was referencing. Weird ideas were the reason I went to art school—at least in the judgment of other people. Why had I accepted their assessment of me? Why was I accepting this woman's? Or even my wife's?

The P.A. placed the prescription pad on the tiny desk and, using her best illegible doctor script, penned the prescription. Then, she handed the paper to my wife, which rubbed me the wrong way. I *was* in the room.

I nearly jumped from my chair, thinking, *Time to go.*

The entire experience had been surreal. I had come here with no expectations other than a blood-pressure check and thermometer insertion, and was leaving after having just been diagnosed by a physician's assistant with depression and possible Bipolar Disorder. In addition, in a rather nonchalant manner, I'd been prescribed a mood-altering drug that would make me 'normal' again.

It occurred to me that if this scenario was normal then 'normal' was the last thing I ever wanted to be.

We paid the twenty-dollar co-pay to the receptionist, and turned towards the elevator. The second the elevator closed and I'd pushed the button for the first floor my wife opened the box of samples.

"Here, take this. We can get started," she said, offering a small white pill.

Again, with the *we* thing.

At least a Muzak version of Patsy Cline's, "Crazy" wasn't playing—although it'd have been fitting.

"We can stop by the pharmacy on the way home and have the prescription filled."

While she spoke, I cringed at the thought of this new daily regimen. To me, it was just another ritual that was required of me, if I was to be acceptable to everyone else in the world.

I took the small white tablet from her fingers like a good boy, popped it into my mouth, and swallowed. One of my many useless talents was the ability to swallow pills without water. It's a gift, really.

Later, I would realize that the real issue at stake was this:

I was becoming disenchanted with and disengaged from what has been called the "consensus reality" of our culture. In the minds of people who bought into that reality—which is that making a lot of money and trudging up the mountain of the so-called American Dream—*should* make you happy and fulfilled.

But what happens if you are the person for whom this is not true? And what if you are taking your cues for what your reality should be from inner and not outer sources?

In my experience, the answer to those questions is: you are labeled with a standard diagnosis and given a box of pills. *There, problem solved.*

My wife stuffed the piece of paper on which the P.A. had written my subscription into her purse and from the look on her face, clearly feeling fully confident. Yet, we were totally unaware that we were setting in motion a series of events neither of us could foresee.

3

THINGS COME APART

IN WHAT SEEMED LIKE the most improbable method to use in the search for happiness—with the exception of seeking a street-corner prostitute or dealer—I grudgingly succumbed to the wishes of my wife and the opinion of a woman who had the authority to make free use of a prescription pad.

What if Wellbutrin could make me feel better? Apparently, it helped a lot of people.

In my case, however, it would prove to be a wrong turn on the path where the inner voice was trying to lead me. I would wonder later why I resisted listening to it. Maybe it's necessary for of some of us to open the wrong doors first. But even here in legal drug land, valuable pieces of learning would emerge.

In her haste to fully answer my questions during the Wellbutrin Q&A session, the P.A. failed to mention something very important about this quest to gain 'normalcy'. Whether she forgot to relate this important tidbit or assumed I would take it upon myself to read the novella neatly folded inside the sample box I would never know. The sheet of contraindications listed in great and horrifying detail the potential side effects of the medication, as well as the do's and don'ts I was to abide while taking it.

I'll just simply state that, regardless of the warnings written in fine print, I loved wine. I was especially fond of red wine. Red wine would put the 'Well' in Wellbutrin.

Barely two weeks after taking my first dose of the new happy pills, I started to feel somewhat different.

Caution, let me reacquaint you with Wind.

I was quite certain, however, that the changes my wife expected to see in my behavior were *not* the effects that she was witnessing. Despite beginning this new daily regimen, the idea of ceasing the consumption of red wine was never a consideration. Whenever we would attend a company function or simply go out for dinner at Olive Garden, the combination of happy pills and alcohol ensured I had no shortage of jokes or qualms about sharing them with strangers. So suddenly she faced the uncertainty of "What is Jeff going to do next?" "What inappropriate comments will he blurt out?" In fairness to me, my random comments were never derogatory or all that inappropriate—usually—but provided levity.

Whether it was the effects of Wellbutrin or the new energy that had begun to free itself inside, I was becoming very free with my opinions and personal truths.

The result, according to her, was that I was starting to tarnish *her* image—and car rides home became increasingly uncomfortable.

In no time, the first big earth tremors began to occur in our relationship. But I was "happy and perky" again. What did she want?

Stick to the point. The important question was—What did you want?

The combination of antidepressants and wine, or vodka or any other alcohol enhanced my state of mind in a strange way. I was getting something I wanted.
I was becoming stronger. I was beginning to speak my truth.
At the same time, I was making a big mistake, seeking escape from the downsides of a major, life transition. But then, you're not always fully aware you're in one.

Yeah, some spiritual road signs would be nice. "Transition in Progress—Stay Alert!"

The self-awareness that I had been struggling with was emerging, and was being outwardly expressed in unexpected ways in the most unexpected places. When I imbibed, I felt I could relate to anyone about anything. It wasn't the alcohol lowering my inhibitions, it was the feeling that I better understood who I was, that I was connected to others and that I felt a vague sense that I was on my way to discovering . . . .
Purpose.
Ever since the new, unusual impressions had first arisen, I'd had a growing sense that I was about to know what I was here in this life to do. Until now, that awareness had always been absent.
My wife seemed even more baffled by what she now labeled as a "rebel" nature. This was more troubling than the 'depressed' guy she'd had on her hands just weeks before. I *still* wasn't the old Jeff she once knew, the one she hoped to reclaim. I was becoming an entirely different "new Jeff"—whoever that was.

It was true. I was evolving and becoming someone that even I didn't recognize. Even though I often blamed it on the alcohol and meds concoction, I somehow knew that was not the truth. Even stone cold sober, I was increasingly resolute in my refusal to abide by conventional rules. Mornings, alone, I stared into the mirror with a disdain for my mock turtleneck and highlighted hair. To everyone else, I still looked fine. To me, the man in the mirror was the crazy one, not the man staring at this socially-acceptable mask.

Much later, I'd conclude that there are many among us who, at some time in our life, can be labeled by the majority opinion as "mentally ill." Listening to the voices that cause us to conform, we can shut down the voice of our authentic self—until a struggle begins between a world that has its own plans for us—a force within that has other, bigger plans. When the war between these two forces finally takes place—whether in our childhood, teenage or adult years—life can get messy.

Mine was about to get messy on a grand scale. Fortunately, with the aid of a very cool ally, my personal strength was growing.

First, there was a subtle change in my life's musical soundtrack.

Before, a song was just a song I'd add to a list of lifetime favorites. Now, I'd hear a song—even one I'd sung along with perhaps hundreds of times—and all at once a lyric would resonate with the exact circumstances happening in my life. It wasn't like I was listening. It was like an energy boosted the lyric and aimed it like a broadcast from beyond specifically to me. I'd heard people in my church or in a men's Bible study say that a given scripture passage had "spoken" to them. I wondered if—except for the words being rock and pop song lyrics—this was in any way like that.

Then there was the rapid change within my marriage.

In an effort to maintain marital harmony, which was becoming difficult, I had adhered to the rules of mental hygiene. Meaning, I had been a good boy—taking my medication as prescribed. The Wellbutrin had not done its part, however, in the *"Let's Make Jeff Normal Again"* campaign.

I couldn't fault my wife for her dismay.

Yes, I was joke-ier, but I wasn't any happier with myself, my life, or thoughts about my future. I still felt trapped—sinking in quicksand and unable to reach the dangled, jungle vine of meaning and purpose. Though I was surrounded by family, neighbors and church 'brethren,' the emptiness and disenchantment grew ever stronger. I *still* felt overlooked, as if something in me still needed to be recognized, and completely alone.

Conversely, my wife's career and sense of worth was on the up-tick. She was shimmying upwards and nearing the uppermost rungs of the corporate ladder. The next rung required us to once again pull up roots and relocate to Virginia, not far from Washington, D.C. Thus far, we'd relocated a few times within North Carolina, with the one exception being one short stint in St. Petersburg, Florida, some years earlier, pre-children.

"This is so exciting! Can you believe that I'm going to be managing the company's entire East Coast portfolio?" my wife enthusiastically exclaimed.

"You've worked hard for it." My next thought was of the tremendous amount of history in the Washington, D.C., area. In terms of our kids' education, this was a great move.

I had to feign enthusiasm, though. To this point, I'd always viewed moving to a new city or state as an adventure. My real gut reaction to the news of this relocation was blasé, which surprised me.

Still, her excitement was genuine, and I was truly happy . . . for *her*. Despite the sharp increase of hours necessary for advancement and the growing strain that it placed on our relationship, I was proud of how far she'd come in her career since we'd first met. She was top-notch at what she did, and this promotion was quite an achievement.

But truthfully, I thought, *Great, time to start packing... again.*

"I need to be there next week. But we have about a month to physically move. God, we have a lot to do, and not much time. I'm really going to need your help. The kids, utilities, movers. Oh! Did I mention that the company is paying for the move? That's a first!"

Wonderful. Will the company also compensate me for uprooting my life again?

Not to be self-centered—though maybe I was, and maybe I needed to be—but with this announcement the impressions I'd been getting months before had become a voice inside, and right now it was fairly shouting,

You are not on your path. Find your path.

What the hell *was* that voice? For all intents and purposes, I'd always thought I was on my path. I was a husband, a father, a church goer, a partial bread winner, and I supposed that my path lay in being faithful to the people I lived to serve—and now, to the bottle full of "take this, and keep being who we need you to be."

That was about to end.

Several months had passed since being 'diagnosed' with depression and probable bipolar disorder. Now everything depended on me staying the course laid out for me. Before we waved goodbye to North Carolina, both the physician's assistant and my wife said, "Jeff, one of the first things you have to do is find a doctor." The instructions were so often repeated and carried such a dire warning I imagined that if I didn't take my little white pill at 9:00 a.m. on a given morning I'd simply drop dead by 10:30. I was not, under any circumstance, to stop taking my medication.

"You could die, or worse," my wife said.

Or worse? What could be worse? I thought. *Oh yeah, the family reunion.*

Okay, don't be a smartass. Your in-laws were inspirational and humorous. A family reunion provided me with more laughter than I'd ever had at a comedy club. They were good people.

As my wife charged off to the office the morning of her announcement, I moved through the house trying to imagine how many packing boxes we'd need, as a verse of Jimmy Buffett's "Changes in Latitudes, Changes in Attitudes" floated through my head and out my lips:

These changes in latitudes, changes in attitudes,
Nothing remains quite the same.
Through all of the islands and all of the highlands,
If we couldn't laugh we would all go insane.

The relocation to Virginia went as smoothly as one would expect after three weeks of frenzied preparation. Dutifully, I searched for a new physician in the brochure that came in our *'Welcome to the Community'* packet. It listed, in alphabetical order, every imaginable service ranging from stump removal to bikini waxing. I couldn't help but snicker when I saw services for plumbing and proctology listed side by side. *That's funny,* I thought. *There's not really much difference in those two professions.*

I called the first general practitioner on the list, but in fact my spirit dropped its head with a sigh.

What the hell.... It's 'just another day in paradise'. I might as well test the water. Buffett be with me.

I made the call and secured the appointment after which I poured a glass of Trader Joe's *'Two Buck Chuck'* Merlot. I told myself I needed to celebrate my intestinal fortitude, and that wine was still my friend, because it played well with Wellbutrin.

There it is, Jeff. You kept avoiding the real issue. You were miles and miles from your true life path. Yeah, maybe your wife and the P.A. pressured you, but you were the one medicating. Why was it so overwhelming and painful to think about changing your life? Chicken...

The "I'm afraid of how big the changes will be" answer didn't surface. At some level, I knew I was caving-in once again. Pushing myself aside so to not upset the apple cart. Inside, I knew that no doctor or medication was going to "fix" me—but the force of long habit provided motivation to do as I'd been instructed.

What if...? What the hell, you never know. Maybe a real doctor can 'fix' me.

I raised my glass and silently toasted the possibilities. *Salud! Here's to getting 'fixed!'*

Three days later I was face to face with another physician's assistant. I wasn't to be seeing a physician that day nor did I consider asking to see a physician. In the back of my mind I had a firm belief that every physician was required by medical law to have me drop my drawers, bend over the white paper-clad table and cough as an E.T.-length finger probed my tonsils. I wasn't really in the mood for that type of intimacy.

The physician's assistant was older than the one who'd earlier labeled me 'depressed'. I appreciated that she looked directly at me as she spoke—possibly because I was alone this time—and she seemed competent. This lady sitting before me, however, knew how to throw a wicked screwball. Without warning, she looked me square in the eyes.

"I insist that you start seeing a psychiatrist. I'm astounded that you've been diagnosed with depression and Bipolar Disorder and have been taking antidepressants without seeing a psychiatrist."

She lowered her hand into the pocket of her white lab coat, pulled out a prescription pad, and ripped a sheet from the top. Flipping the paper over, she scribbled the name and number of a psychiatrist.

Why is she so intense?

The seriousness in her voice raised a host of questions. I was also in disbelief and taken completely off-guard.

"Take this, and give him a call to arrange an appointment." The words sounded like orders, not a suggestion. "Also, I'm giving you a refill for Wellbutrin, but if it isn't working anymore—"

I wanted to shout, *It never did work.*

"—this doctor is excellent. He'll be able to better assess what the best treatment options for your condition will be." The treatment of mental illness is a bit out of my league."

Hold on a second—my condition? Now I definitely have Bipolar Disorder? What the. . . ? This isn't why I came here. I'm just need a prescription refill so I don't die at 9:00 A.M. next Wednesday. Oh yeah, and to make my wife happy. Wait ... mental illness treatment is out of your league? Then why am I talking to you in the first place?

In that exact moment of upset and agitation, however, I felt a strange wave of comfort wash through me. A sense that everything was going to be okay. I suddenly felt safe and . . .

 . . . *not alone.*

It was a palpable sense of . . . fullness . . . solidity . . . presence. As if someone was with me, right beside me. I felt filled from the center of my being with warmth and lightness.

Possibly for the first time, after living so many years up in my head and not in my heart, *I paid attention to the feeling that overflowed from my own heart center.* Something was awakening there. That was a wonderful feeling.

I took the piece of paper from the P.A.'s hand, not sure if I would use it or toss it. A hulking dose of a new reality had just made itself known.

As she continued talking I was barely listening. Instead, I became aware of some dimension of reality larger than my little slice of life. Before today, I had been seated—popcorn in hand, feet propped on the seat in front of me—watching the coming attractions. Now, the curtains opened a bit more. I wondered where this journey would take me as the main attraction started to flicker onscreen—titled, "The Adventure of Your Life—You Ain't Seen Nothin' Yet."

I left the doctor's office with mixed emotions and scrambled thoughts. After the infilling moment, I felt myself settling back into the person I'd been before going in. Well, not exactly. I'd had a taste of something bigger than the life I was living.

C'mon, buddy, it's up to you. Are you going to go on the adventure or not? Don't wuss out on me!

Settling into the car, I felt a bit uncertain.

I buckled in, fired up the engine, and reached to turn on the stereo. The channel was set to a mellow R&B channel that my wife preferred. As I wasn't in a mellow R&B frame of mind, I found a classic rock channel and cranked up the volume, ready to immerse myself in song. Instead, I was boxed in the ears with commercials.

Ugh. Sell, sell, sell. Make that money!

Ten minutes of hard sell clogged the air between just two four-minute songs.

Now my hearing seemed more acute. I listened to the ads with a different set of ears. I heard something in the sales pitches other than, "*Hurry! This offer is available for a limited time!*" and "*This weekend only! Drive away in a new car with no money down!*" I heard impassioned pleas—directed at everyone—especially those whose priorities were focused on getting the best deal and having the best 'stuff.'

Rather than judging "those people"—I saw myself as an extreme example of *those* people.

That moment of raw clarity exposed one truth about who I was right at that moment. I had a ton of 'stuff.' There was the closet, crammed full of designer clothing, a collection of wristwatches—the Rolex Submariner being the crown jewel—a Brett Favre autographed football, my 62-inch-screen TV. (I did enjoy a few Super Bowl Sundays sitting in front of that screen.) The list went on and on. I had all of this 'stuff', and suddenly it none of it mattered.

It was like the larger self I'd encountered in the doctor's office was looking at a smaller version of me. One who was attached to images and roles and stuff just as much as anybody else. No wonder I was afraid of letting go of it. To this point, it largely defined me.

If I'm not my career, and I'm not my wife's career, and I'm more than a dad, and I'm not my stuff. . . ?

I looked at my image in the rearview mirror.

Sitting on the bridge of my nose were $200 Oakley sunglasses. My body was clad head to toe in clothes that were the latest, most fashionable and trendiest available.

I'm nothing more than a walking, talking product placement for Oakley, Banana Republic, and professional teeth whitening.

The guy staring back at me was the product of years of church teaching, societal expectations and the opinionated ideals of others. I was a group-effort creation.

Now, that image was coming apart, like an old puzzle falling off the table. Who would replace the old me?

The truth was, I had stepped into a rapidly moving process—one in which the old me was coming down, so that a new one could emerge. At that moment, I only felt as if forces deep inside me were pulling me in pieces, and I couldn't stop it from happening.

DJ, cue the soundtrack.

The first tune in queue following the commercial break was by Bon Jovi. I'd heard the song only two or three times—having never been a big Bon Jovi fan—and had never paid much attention to the lyrics. That day, the song grabbed me by the soul.

I pulled into the parking lot of an outlet mall, and stopped the car as the lyrics to "It's My Life" caused my body to vibrate:

This ain't a song for the broken-hearted
No silent prayer for the faith-departed,
I ain't gonna be just a face in the crowd.
You're gonna hear my voice
When I shout it out loud,
It's my life
It's now or never
I ain't gonna live forever
I just want to live while I'm alive

My heart is like an open highway.
Like Frankie said,
I did it my way,
I just wanna live while I'm alive
It's my life.

Right then, those words dramatically altered the course of my life. Every truth I'd ever believed was about to be challenged.

I had two distinct feelings: a twinge of fear coupled with a surge of strength.

Little did I know that I was also stepping out onto my own path. A huge change was on the way—way more than I bargained for.

4
THE SHOW

ASIDE FROM SEEING A PSYCHIATRIST, there were no longer any certainties: my marriage, career, sense of self, and entire future had grouped themselves and formed a huge, boldfaced question mark. My spiritual trek was taking me on a detour, and I didn't have a clue where I was headed, but the moment of upheaval was about to take place.

Driving my family to church on one typical Sunday morning, I was oblivious to what was about to occur, a revelation that would come with a subtlety akin to Wile E. Coyote dropping a huge box of ACME caustic lye from a cliff. Whereas the roadrunner always dodged the box, it would land this morning squarely on someone's head.

We were now attending a Methodist church in northern Virginia, and as we parked and ushered ourselves inside the church, it faintly occurred to me that a whole lifetime of experiences—good, bad, and ugly—were all in some way associated with religious teachings.

Granted, not every Christian I knew was taught as a child that they were lost and going to hell unless they *(fill in the blank here)* accepted Jesus as Lord and Savior, partook of the graces offered by the Church, engaged in "soul winning," etc. but that was the message I'd heard. I was taught not to trust myself because I and everyone else had a "fallen nature" and we were selfish to the core. We were also not to trust ourselves to choose our own path in life because God had a "perfect plan" for us. I'd begun to think that, so far, that perfect plan looked suspiciously just like the so-called "American Dream." Our place was to ask for direction and do as we are told.

Use Jesus' life as an example of how to live. Yeah, ok. That's impossible . . . he was God in the flesh, right? Therefore, he was perfect. How the hell do I follow that example? Then again . . . he did flip some tables out of anger . . .

And here I was, awakening to a voice that was beginning to rebel against this so-called American Dream life I'd been "blessed with". What if I was still just an "unsaved" rebel?

As we fast-walked through the church lobby—because we were late, as usual—there was more.

This morning, as was true many other Sundays, I'd been more and more aware that these teachings brought with them unanswered questions and gnawing uncertainties—about things like prayers that were never answered, tragic senseless deaths, terrible suffering. There was also a veritable Pandora's Box of protocols, and forced feelings of gratitude for—well, everything. I was to be grateful for the food on my plate, Duke University's repeat championship performance, and "the positives" that come along with being vertically challenged. In short, I was troubled by "the formula", which went like this: all you had to do was pray, ask for forgiveness, and believe that Jesus died for your sins, and afterwards, life would be golden and filled with unicorns and rainbows. Okay, I was getting cynical, I admit. But after you were "set free" you were fine—fine, that is, for as long as you continued to adhere to religious protocol *and be grateful*. If you were not grateful, the blessings would cease.

Sort of like you'd ticked-off Santa Claus. I must have owned a coal mine.

Part of the protocol was to smile and grin as I entered church and greeted everyone, a simple thing which was difficult for me to do this morning. I found myself thinking, ironically, sarcastically, *Smile, dammit! You're saved now. You should be happy and full of grace and gratitude.*

Today, like so many Sunday mornings in the recent past, I just wasn't "pickin' up what they'd been puttin' down."

Now the doors to the sanctuary were being closed by the ushers and the opening strains of a hymn were being pounded out on the piano.

"Welcome!" a smiling, older gentleman said enthusiastically. "You *just barely* made it before the service. Thank goodness."

Lucky us.

Making our way quickly down the aisle, I noticed that nearly everyone was smiling. Big, Cheshire cat smiles, accompanied by chatter. I didn't feel like smiling, and I died inside a little bit as I put one out there. My eyes darted from left to right as we looked for a seat. "Damn, it's crowded today," I whispered to my wife. "Damn," or forms of the word, was used throughout the Bible, so I didn't have any second thoughts at having used it in church. "Sonofabitch," however, would have elicited a glare from my wife, triggering a post-church 'discussion.'

Finding "our pew"—next to the aisle in case a kid had to use the bathroom—we squeezed into place like Star-Kist sardines cramming into a pop-top can. Grabbing a hymnal, I sat back and took in the simple, yet tastefully adorned sanctuary.

On the stage up front, the altar was draped in a brilliant purple cloth, and in front of it three tables covered in white were arranged in "U" formation. Today, the tables held baskets piled high with bread—symbolizing "the body of Christ"—and cups of grape juice for the "blood."

It was Communion Sunday, but I didn't focus on the symbolic ceremony and its props. Instead I found myself staring around the sanctuary. It seemed that once again some voice inside me was trying to speak, but I couldn't hear what it was saying.

I realized it would take extra effort today to hide the effects of disagreements and frustrations encountered during the drive to church. We would all have to smile big today. And look perfectly happy to be here.

C'mon, I brow-beat myself. *It's just church. What's the big deal? It's not a big deal—just sing. Make a joyful noise, damnit.*

Still, I felt like an ocean creature that had outgrown its shell, and now was trying to crawl back into it.

When had I started losing enthusiasm for this whole deal? Was it the day that I'd stood in the bedroom, looking through the window and concluding that there was so much missing from my life that years of church had failed to provide? Possibly it was the Sunday afternoon earlier that year—an afternoon spent at my in-law's house after having attended church. I'd watched my father-in-law nearly panic as one of the church brethren came up the front walk to the door, causing him to scramble to hide his glass of wine. What would the brethren think if he saw one of the church elders half-snockered on a Sunday afternoon? Numerous events like this all flooded through the theater of my mind, any collection of them likely for my loss of enthusiasm.

Hey, those events were to thank, not to blame, for your loss of Sunday canned-service enthusiasm. Huh. Maybe I learned something after all.

That was it. It felt canned. Rote. Hamster on a wheel kind of thing. In my mind, I was already back at the house, or better yet, having a post-church meal at my favorite Thai restaurant and enjoying a glass or three of Cabernet Sauvignon.

I checked my watch. Ten minutes in—maybe an hour to go, or a little more since we had to do the Communion line shuffle today.

After the sermon, we would all stand, form a single-file line, and shuffle up to the front of the sanctuary. There, we'd accept the body in the form of tiny, broken-up pieces of King's Hawaiian bread, receive a blessing, shuffle to the left, dunk the body into a goblet of grape juice representing blood, receive another blessing, and then mutter, "Thanks be to God." Then, it was a quick shuffle back to the pew to watch the others, although the pious were expected to bow in prayer after returning to the pew. Easy-peasy.

The Sunday Shuffle—a mandatory dance much like the Electric Slide at a wedding reception.

As I thought about Communion, that's when the inner voice started to become clear again.

Sure, Communion was a simple ritual, but for me it raised an irrational fear that maybe I didn't take the ceremony as seriously as I should. Communion is a solemn ceremony, one in which you're supposed to experience and express gratitude—there was that demand again—that Jesus died for me and everyone else. From the very first time I'd taken part in this ritual, however, I'd never quite known how I should feel about it. Should I be happy that Jesus, in a symbolic way, passed on his body and blood to me personally, or should I feel sad that this was a reenactment of Jesus' actions before he was nailed to a cross? Afterwards, should I continue to feel that familiar guilt at having received this blessing despite my sinful actions of the past week? Or even the past hour as my wife and I bitched at each other on the way to church—again?

In truth, all those feelings were combined into one knotted ball of holy Christmas lights that, if verbalized, would say, "I understand, but I don't get it."

Okay. Too much thinking. I shoved the questions to the back of my mind. Today was the first time our son would be participating in Communion, and I knew that he would want to know what the entire ceremony meant. I needed to be an example of piety.

We were halfway through the opening hymn now—usually, a barn-burner, meant to raise group enthusiasm from "ugh, it's morning" to "rock concert" level. The pianist and "praise band" kicked it into high gear and for me they might as well have been playing Boston's "Foreplay". That's where my mind took me.

Just dandy. Another so-so opening act before the headliner.

As we belted it out, I couldn't help but notice the very animated lady with the choir, who would throw her hands into the air, look upwards and yelp out a random, "Hallelujah!" I was reminded of televangelists and the movie "Sister Act" at the same time.

Call me judgmental . . . .

Okay, you're judgmental. You're human, after all.

. . . but it felt like a performance. And if it wasn't for anyone else, it had become one for me.

This spectacle was followed by a host of speakers, committee spokespersons, and a weekly update from the church treasurer. It seemed that despite a growing congregation, the church was still behind on the monthly and yearly budget goals. Had I really showered, shaved, and driven my kids—foot-dragging all the way—to church to hear about budget short-falls?

Afterwards, the minister offered a prayer, and *ba-da-bing, ba-da-boom*, the ushers holding baskets appeared at the ends of each pew. Oh, the guilt and shame I'd feel on those Sundays when I had no cash or checkbook. Others sitting further downline, waiting for the basket, must have thought the worst on those days, when we had nothing but a business card or IOU to place in the basket.

Another hymn or two, and now it was time for the monthly ritual of Communion. I had taken part in this ritual in some form since I was a kid, and I'd always wondered about those who didn't fall in line to shuffle forward and take a morsel of bread and dip it in the cup of juice. My understanding from an early age was that this was a requirement, and I supposed that the ones who remained seated were either visitors, or they were shy, or new to the faith.

Those were my thoughts about the seated strangers. I had other misgivings, about myself. I wondered if accepting Jesus as my savior had really taken hold since, as I'd been reminded countless times—

Did I mention this already?

—by preachers, Sunday school teachers, televangelists, relatives and neighbors that we were all sinners, and Hell was full of sinners who didn't accept Jesus as their personal savior—*as well as those who had accepted Jesus then failed to lead a "godly" life.*

My shirt collar always felt a little tight at that last part.

I blame the necktie.

Today, as my son and I neared the front of the church, I saw that the minister was doling out the bread and that the choir member who was earlier reaching for heaven during the hymns was holding the cup of juice. I did a back step. The woman was wearing a freakishly broad smile, while lavishly blessing everyone who partook of the offering. She was the poster child for smiling.

As we inched closer and closer to the bread bearer, I watched my son. His face and demeanor had become more serious. The nervous smile was there, but his silence was a sure sign that he was feeling more than a bit insecure. I felt sure that his thoughts were the same mine had been at that age.

The shuffling had stopped as we were now standing before the pastor—Jesus' chosen deliverer of the bread—whose smile was inviting and words were gentle. He bent to offer the bread to my son, whose hands were cupped to receive the offering. And what else would a young boy do if handed a large chunk of King's Hawaiian loaf? Yes, he started to pop it into his mouth.

I bent and whispered, "No, wait. Don't eat it yet."

After receiving a blessing from the pastor along with a gentle pat on the head, my son shuffled to his left and waited as I received my own bread and blessing.

When we shuffled our way towards the cup, the "Hallelujah!"

lady was waiting, cup in hand, with the neon smile that shouted, *"Joy! Love! Forgiveness!"*

Bending over to lower the cup to my son's level, she whispered, "Just dip the bread into the cup."

I watched as he awkwardly held the crumbling piece of bread in his fingers. It reminded me of how a kid would approach a stranger's dog before petting it—slowly and with trepidation.

And then, the *unthinkable* happened.

My son dropped his bread into the cup. It was as if a slow-motion action sequence were taking place on a wide screen in a packed theater. Whether he unintentionally dropped the bread or it simply broke apart as he dipped into the cup, the body of Christ was now floating in a cup of juice.

He's a kid. No big deal, I thought. It wasn't the first time I'd approached the cup and noticed floaters.

He looked up at me, obviously embarrassed, but with an innocent, *oops* kind of smile.

I placed my hands on his shoulders in a reassuring gesture and looked down to say, "S'ok. No big deal."

The moment after I'd reassured him, however, I looked up—and it was very apparent that my son's failure to control his bread *was* a big deal. A huge deal.

The woman who was holding the cup of love and salvation—who moments before had been shouting "Hallelujah"—was glaring at my son with a look of pure disgust, as if he had spit or picked his nose during the Last Supper.

What you're seeing is a veneer of religious ritual and performance, without the power of spiritual reality, said the voice inside. That look and that moment I'd never forget.

This time I heard the voice clearly and distinctly, so strongly I blinked.

So, you're telling everyone you're not crazy—but you're hearing voices . . . . Right. Right.

We made our way back to our seats. Our son went directly for the crayon that he'd had in his pocket, and began doodling. As for me, I tried to focus on the hymn we were singing—*O! the Deep, Deep Love of Jesus*—but I couldn't. As Communion ended, I watched the woman who had expressed anything but Christ-like love towards my son return to her place in the choir and again throw her hands in the air with her same perma-smile as before, while looking to heaven and again shouting, "Hallelujah!"

Hallelujah? Go tell it on the mountain, lady.

For me, it was as if the whole atmosphere of the sanctuary had gone flat.

Later, after the service concluded, as was customary, we all filed out of the church Gathering Space, smiling, shaking hands, and exchanging pleasantries. As luck would have it I came face to face with the choir lady again—smiling mask back in place. I did not see acceptance, as her outstretched hand unsuccessfully tried to shake my pocketed hand. I did not hear a genuineness in her "Have a blessed day" farewell remark. All I could continue to see—was it me being judgmental, or suddenly keenly observant?—was crystal clear reflection of shallow religiosity.

We got in the car and headed to our favorite Thai restaurant.

Thank God for Thai food and an after-church serving of cabernet.

The shift that began back in church was not stopping. My mind was now churning over the repetitive, soulless nature of so many aspects of my lifetime's worth of experience with organized religion. The passing of the plate. The constant need for money. The many sermons and references to sin and the dire consequences of living a sinful life or one not "sold out to" and "serving Jesus" twenty-four-seven.

For all the rhetoric, though, I didn't know very many people who were "sold out" for Jesus. I knew more "sell outs"—truthfully, myself included. I had witnessed so much religious hypocrisy in myself and ninety-nine percent of my church brethren and sister-en by this point in my life that the utter shallowness of religious veneer was the first of those long-unexpressed truths to make its way up from the subterranean depths of my mind.

We drove home, my wife chattering away with the kids, and me feeling like I was on tilting ground. It wasn't just the religious circumstances of that morning that bothered me. I now felt like a chasm was opening between me and my whole religious past.

The play-acting at church was screaming silently from within my own family—and in the ministers and so-called God-fearing adults I'd known in other cities and other churches. Most startling, I saw it in myself.

You know that they say, if you point a finger of blame, four are pointing right back at ya.

The sobering truth that kept shaking me was this: the spiritual aspect of religion I'd lived or tried to live was lost in the rituals, and a constant struggle to be "acceptable to God." And we who said we believed in the unconditional love of God—that we were accepted by him in the name of Jesus—in truth relied upon everything else for spiritual "validation". We said we were all about grace, but in fact we were all about good works and about conformity to a religious norm. Just as I'd experienced when looking at our nice, upper-middle class community and at our career paths—the same need to conform to everybody else's expectations was alive but not well here in my religious community.

All this nearly knocked the wind out of me. Because there was that voice *again*—not quite my own voice but another, strongly, sounding in my head, saying, *Enough trying to conform to consensus reality—the one that's all about money and success and the one that's all about religious veneers.*

For the rest of the day my perspective continued to shift, as I saw church and religion itself in an entirely new light. My feelings rocketed around like the little blue sphere in a racquetball game. I felt sick in my soul. I felt I'd been misled and manipulated my entire life. And I felt angry that I'd bought into and played the game.

There was more to what was happening to me, though, than feeling manipulated, strong as that feeling was. Sitting in church that morning, the whole scene playing out in front of me had gone flat and gray in my mind's-eye, like it was nothing more than a flat curtain or one of my perfectly pressed bed sheets. Behind the screen of this "spiritual play", greater realities were going on. How to get to them, though? That was not what the play was about. The play was about the *play*.

I was left with the strong sense that something bigger lay behind all this—not just my neighborhood and the canned church service—all of this. Everything we can see. The sad thing was, the very things that could pull back the curtain, like church services, actually block us from seeing, experiencing, and knowing these realities.

During the days that followed, I made the decision: No more pretending to be "saved". The fact was, I'd never felt that "spiritual liberation" I'd so often been promised if only I would "give my life and cares over to Jesus." Never. In fact, there had always been superficiality, held in place by play-acting—as far back as I could remember. And with it, a feeling of being trapped into religious behavior patterns prescribed by our particular brand of spirituality.

Because I lived in North Carolina and as a kid was raised southern-style, I went to church on Sundays. I didn't have much say in the matter. It was just a given, an unspoken rule, and I was a kid with no other choice. My family belonged to a Methodist church, a relatively harmless and liberal wing of the Christian faith, especially when compared to other Christian denominations. In one sense, we didn't try to hide much. There is an old joke that goes: "If you see a Baptist and a Methodist in a liquor store, how can you tell which one is the Methodist?" Answer: "The Methodist won't try to duck and hide as he's browsing the whiskey section."

That joke summed up neatly, at least in my eyes, how Methodism wasn't as strict a discipline as many other religious denominations. Still, Methodists were mired in other underlying hypocrisies and they had their fair share of ceremonies and rituals. I'm not singling out Baptists or anyone else for ridicule. I'm only saying that I tended to look at Methodism as the Sprite Zero of Christianity. Not too sweet, light and bubbly, and briefly refreshing.

Being treated to this light skim over the surface of spirituality began way back when I was young. I saw that now.

As a child, before the Big Show in the sanctuary, my Sunday morning required my presence in Sunday school. Oh, how I loved Sunday school! There were snacks, juice, coloring books and the eventual story time, during which we heard over and over about Jonah in the belly of a whale or Noah rounding up two of every living creature on earth and loading them onto a huge, handmade boat. Story time was always followed by time to create a prop from the story, using macaroni, yarn, and Elmer's glue.

The stories were always entertaining to me. I did not actually believe that a man was swallowed by a whale and was miraculously belched out soon after. Other stories seemed just as implausible. The Bible was chock-full of stories. The front of the Good Book, the part that starts at the Beginning was represented in Sunday school by the stories of Adam and Eve with that wily snake, Noah, Jonah, Job and David's slaying Goliath. And nobody seemed worried if I took any of these tales literally. Which, in a way, was a good thing.

Later, however, I encountered stories about God's horrifying violence—ordering even women and infants to be slaughtered, and demanding that severe punishments he meted out, like stoning and torture. And then there was the carnality of some of those early Jewish leaders. When I was a kid, these tales had been either gingerly told or skipped over.

There were hints of depth, though.

The stories about Jesus were the ones that really kept me captivated. The Resurrection, immaculate conception, his walking on water, the Crucifixion. These stories and his teachings through parables seemed real to me. I emotionally place myself into those stories. Sure, the Jesus of those stories was an adult man. But the man was first a kid, and that was where I was most easily able to relate. Between the virgin birth and his turning water into wine, I could see him being just like me. Rambunctious, curious, rowdy, rebellious, adventurous, carefree . . . just a kid. I imagined he'd be a kid who'd hunt for salamanders or ride bikes with me after school.

It was when I was told that Jesus was God in human form, though, I had started questioning.

Was it true that he was really that unique—God in human form? A few other religions claimed the same thing about their gods. Or was Jesus a man who had tapped into a spiritual power of some kind? What about those miracles? Again, he was not the only one with special powers. Jewish and Christian holy men and women, Hindu sadhus, Buddhist yogis, Sufi mystics, and Native American medicine men and women—all performed miracles. These thoughts and questions had rumbled around silently inside me for a long time. Now they were unsettling all the certainty I'd been offered since I was a kid that there was only "one path to God."

The Sundays that followed found my heart, mind, and soul elsewhere. Disenchantment was increasingly evident to my wife and children. This meant that it was also evident to others in attendance—something that didn't sit well with my wife. Now, when we were to offer others the pre-planned, canned "greeting," I stayed firmly in place, ass to pew, hands on knees, watching what I now thought of as "the show".

During these shows, I reflected on my life. I thought of how profoundly church and religion had influenced me as a child, and chafed at the shallowness I'd seen.

I thought of the fully stocked minibar at home that was enjoyed by my parents and their friends on the occasional Saturday night—then seeing them the following Sunday morning at church, singing *"How Great Thou Art,"* and smiling the smile of tee-totaling purity. *They were also human beings. Loving, wonderfully supportive parents and human beings.*

Okay, so imbibing when you're not supposed to is one thing. There were darker sides to the world I'd grown up in. Not terrible things, but grosser dishonesties.

I thought of my grandfather, who I'd barely known before he'd passed away. I pictured the many church directory pictures I'd seen with him smiling and huddled close to my grandmother, my mom, and my uncle. They were images of a happy family and a good, god-fearing man. What wasn't apparent was his love of alcohol. Nor did I know about his own guilt. I'd later learn that although he was never abusive when drinking, he would often come home driving a new car. Gifting a car was both his peace offering for the family and his symbol of atonement.

Then, of course, there was "the show".

Why need to be dressed in my Sunday finest to go to church? The answer that had been programmed into me was that God is a stickler and damn strict when it comes to appearance in "His House." *No suit, no salvation.*

All this, this shift in *seeing* let loose inside my head. I thought of those teachings and influences, the discreet and indiscreet hypocrisies I'd witnessed for so many years . . . and how I'd allowed them to play such a large role in creating the man I had become. My entire life, my identity, from childhood to that moment when I knew "this ain't right" seemed to me to be filled with compost.

As the weeks passed, my Sunday morning appearances at church tapered off. Occasionally my wife and kids would also skip Sunday services. *A sign of solidarity, perhaps?* No, I felt the pain on those occasions. Subtle words of admonishment meant to elicit guilt and fear of hell can do that. Though most Sundays I was strongly urged to accompany them to the show, I remained resolute in my refusal to participate.

I did not know it at the time, but my old way of seeing and believing was being wiped clean in preparation for a new way to take its place.

Fortunately, despite the festering tension between myself and my wife and my distance from my spiritual community, my soul spoke to me with a tone of reassurance that I was okay—that I was finally free to question.

Soon that voice would begin urging me to take a detour from the highway I'd long traveled. Very soon, I'd take a sharp turn in my search for answers—and find myself in a place without a map or GPS.

5

MARCHING INTO A WAR ZONE

SLOWLY MY EYES WERE OPENING to a bigger reality. The word "*awakening*" is an understatement: my experience was more of a swift kick in the crotch than an *'awakening'*. Numerous events were pivotal in defining who I was becoming—a spiritual, self-aware person. Those moments came flying at me in rapid fire succession. Each one seemed to be outfitted with a laser sight that was aimed directly at my soul.

One of those defining moments was like cannon fire, and got my full attention.

Another of those routine, church-centered Sunday mornings arrived, and that day, post-church, as we made the twenty-minute drive from the Thai restaurant back to our house, I decided that a conversation was in order.

Heck, the time seemed right to me. How was I supposed to know I should have worn a flak-jacket?

I initiated the discussion by expressing dismay—so to speak—saying I felt as if the church didn't need us there and that no one ever noticed that we'd been in attendance on any given Sunday. There was no doubt in my mind that my own presence at church had for a very long time gone unnoticed—at least the *authentic* Jeff.

I said, "My attendance isn't necessary. I prepaid my fare for a one-way ticket to Hell years ago."

You said that in front of your kids, didn't you?

"What are you talking about?" was the response from the front passenger seat.

"You really need to ask? My voucher for the Pearly Gates has been revoked so many times that Saint Peter has me on a blacklist. Your name is probably on there, too. We lived in sin, remember? That's a big no-no right there." I crooked my right arm and made a tight fist. "But, who knows? I'm keepin' hope alive!"

Without waiting for a response, I unloaded my new sense of conviction.

"We don't even *need* to go to church. They give us envelopes. Hell, they even *mail* the envelopes to the house. We can save money on gas, pay for a stamp, and mail God's money directly to His house. Why do we need to be there?"

Our children were buckled up in the back seat, their faces indicating that they were very interested in hearing my wife's response.

"Jeff, we go to church because we are Christians. We tithe because we need to give back to God for the blessing's he's given us. Plus, we go to church so that the kids can learn to live their lives like Jesus expects them to live—you know, as Christians," she calmly replied.

I knew that her answer was tailor-made for the kids' ears.

With a curt tone, she leaned over and whispered, "You're being very disrespectful. You're not setting a good example for the kids and you're pissing me off by making fun of God."

I certainly had not made fun of God, but the shallow "churchy culture" we'd been splashing around in no longer felt deep enough to get the tops of my feet wet.

There is a reality far deeper than what you've experienced, my man.

The voice again.

A bit annoyed with her textbook answer, I pressed on. I believed that our kids should be allowed to hear my questions and have the freedom to chime-in with their own answers and opinions if they wanted.

"Why don't you and the kids start going on Sundays? I can sit at home and read the Bible or watch Billy Graham in my underwear. Better yet, I can do some online shopping. Then, I'll know exactly what I'm getting for my money."

The kids chuckled.

My wife did not.

"It's a no-brainer. We can just mail the check on Friday mornings. They won't know we weren't there. When they run the numbers on Monday morning, our weekly donation will be in the mix. That way, on those Sundays like today, when we don't have cash, we won't feel like we shortchanged God, and I won't get the stink-eye when I hand the plate to the usher."

There was no response from the passenger seat, and I continued to finally vent my long-held frustrations.

"Since we didn't have any cash today, next week when the finance committee guy steps up and tells everyone how the church is way off-budget and that they might have to scrap the Family Living Center, we won't have to endure an hour of feeling like everybody is looking at us and thinking that we're cheap assholes. I can hear them now. 'Pssst, look at the Brunks. They didn't give five bucks to God today. God's problems will never go away now.' I never knew how desperately God needs cash 'til now, did you? I think we already owe something like, oh, three million dollars—give or take."

I felt the need to add a touch of snarkiness in making my point.

The silence from the passenger seat was a bit louder.

I was expecting a nod of the head or a remark indicating agreement.

Changing gears slightly, I continued—knowing that my wife would eventually acknowledge the truth and agree with me.

She has to, I thought. She was an intelligent, business-savvy woman. We'd been married and going to church together for eighteen years. No way she wasn't aware of what was happening, I reasoned. She got annoyed if the bedsheets hadn't been ironed with crisp, straight creases. How could she not be annoyed at the weekly attempts to elicit sympathy and more cash for the Family Living Center—with basketball hoops?

In one sense, I was on the right track. Jumping feet first into greater spiritual realities has a cost, and it's much more than a few bucks tossed in a collection plate. It costs everything, as I would learn. At the moment, I was too focused on the religious veneer I was seeing and how thin it was. It sounded like I was just bashing religiosity or our church.

Well, you were. At least, on the surface that's what it surely sounded like, don't ya think?

More than that, I was trying to articulate the hunger that

was awakening in me—for depth and reality. I could sense it was there, but couldn't get to it. Now the frustration I'd felt with the American-Dream veneer had spread to the world of religious veneers.

My wife's silence prodded me to ask another question.

You just didn't know when to zip the lip, did ya?

"Doesn't it bother you that almost every week, the first fifteen or twenty minutes of the service are nothing more than pleas for money?"

Her head swiveled in my direction. A quick glance showed her displeasure with my question. She then looked quickly to the back seat. The kids were occupied with whatever toy or game each had carried with them that day. Then her head swung forward, and she made it a point to avoid looking at me, but sat in silence looking directly ahead.

I did not see what was happening. Truly, I did not. As I was slowly drifting from the religiosity of my upbringing, a rift was widening between my wife and me.

My questions and comments surely had elements of humor and snarkiness embedded within them. Having been married for so many years, my wife was used to it. I was the Costello to her Abbott. Right now, though, I was purposely being ignored. But I continued.

"Be honest, don't you get annoyed while everyone smiles and laughs and sings, as if they have no problems? I'll bet at least half of the men go home today and masturbate while watching porn or throw back a six pack or two while watching golf. Half the women will get together to play *Bunko*, drink Peach Schnapps, and gossip about who had Botox injections."

No response. No looks. Nothing at all.

"Odds are pretty good that quite a few men and women got pissed off at another driver this morning, yelled and gave the 'You're Number One' middle finger on the way to church. I'm pretty sure that if we didn't do that same thing this morning, we've done it on other Sunday mornings. I know for a fact that it happens at some point during the other six days of the week. I guess other drivers don't realize that we're running late for church on Sunday. 'Hey! Get the hell out of the way! We're gonna be late getting to God's house!'"

A barely audible "ahem" came from the passenger seat.

She's about to admit her annoyance. She's going to agree with me, I thought.

"All it takes to put things right with Jesus," I barreled ahead, "is to go to church, bow our heads, pray for forgiveness, thank Jesus, and promise to do better. *BAM.* It's just like hitting the restart button on the computer. Of course, at 12:01 p.m. all bets are off—until next Sunday anyway." I was smiling and looking for a reaction, sure that she'd come over to my side.

Instead, the silence was becoming thicker and more painful.

My contributions to this rather one-sided conversation, I now realized, were becoming a rant, one born out of my frustration with being ignored combined with more than forty years of questions, and—now—a deep weariness with religions' attempts to control my life and everyone else's.

"If you think about it, no matter where we've lived or which churches we've attended, most members acted, spoke, and even *freakin'* smiled the exact same way—like holy clones."

My wife continued to listen, grimacing slightly.

"I've been in sales for several years, I know the game. I'm not saying that everyone we've ever met in church showed up just to put on a happy face for a couple of hours. I'm only saying that on Sundays, in any church we've ever attended for any length of time, most of the people who seem to be filled with joy because they're on a first name basis with the Holy Ghost aren't genuine."

I couldn't stop myself now.

"I'll guarantee you that the Holy Ghost is nowhere to be found most Saturday nights and on Monday mornings the only 'joy' most church people have will be the dishwashing liquid under the kitchen sink. Haven't you noticed the 'fakeness' and posing? Hell, we're the same way—except that we don't buy Joy dishwashing liquid."

I stopped speaking when I noticed from the corner of my eye my wife's head turning in my direction. Her gaze was firmly affixed to my right side profile.

"What do you mean, '*We're* the same way?'"

Uh oh.

Her question lacked a calm, quizzical tone. It was combative and, as I was prone to do to diffuse a potential confrontation, I laughed a little. I honestly believed for a moment that she was kidding around.

She wasn't. The clear sound of anger in her voice confused me. My brain frantically scrambled to find the words that would possibly better clarify my feelings and observations—words that could allow her to better connect in her own way with what I was saying. But I wasn't quite prepared to give a rebuttal.

"Well, uh,"—I grasped for words, examples—"think about it a minute. What did we do this past week? I don't recall sitting around the kitchen table to study the Bible. I *do* vaguely remember nailing the 'Carlton Dance' to *'It's Not Unusual'* on the patio with what's-her-name from across the street late last night during the neighborhood barbecue at our place. Last night was fun, wasn't it? I don't even like the 'neighborhood get together' thing, but Jesus knew what he was doing when he turned water into wine that day. I know that I sure as hell didn't feel like coming to church with a hangover to sing, smile, and pretend that life is perfect—and I highly doubt that you did either. Am I right?"

In the silence that followed this time, I could *feel* her response. The atmosphere in the front seat was warm and getting warmer, tense, and prickly. Waiting for her response had the same feel to it that one might have while watching a volcano start to heave and shudder. Yet, I also knew that *she knew* I was right.

I also knew her well enough to know that she wasn't about to admit that I was spot-on with my assessment.

The conversation, such as it was, abruptly ended as we turned into the neighborhood. We sat in silence in our driveway while waiting for the garage door to open. I slowly eased the vehicle into the garage, coming to a gentle stop.

To the right was my pride and joy—an olive-green Hummer H3. It was, as always, clean, waxed on the outside and spotless inside. The vanity license plate I'd chosen simply spelled out 'B00GER.' The name seemed appropriate given the color. I'd chosen the name, much to the initial dismay of my wife. That was the reason we mostly drove my wife's black Mercedes Benz. That and the fact the real spelling of Mercedes Benz is *S-t-a-t-u-s S-y-m-b-o-l.*

Hey, you were still driving it, man. You weren't that disenchanted with the shallow world of the American Dream quite yet.

As we entered the house from the garage I had the sudden feeling that my words of disenchantment and feelings of being misled, fooled, snookered, and manipulated by the church were taken as personal assaults on my wife, her family, my kids, Christianity, any friends we'd ever made—also the Pope, Jesus, the chairman of the church finance committee, and all of humankind. I felt as if I'd struck more nerves than a kid with a twitch, trying to play the game *"Operation."*

It was way bigger than that.

Inside the house, the kids bolted in opposite directions. Our son, an avid gamer, headed directly for the Xbox, and our teenaged daughter darted to the confines of her room two levels upstairs—intent on not being seen for the remainder of the day.

My wife and I climbed the single flight of stairs to the main level of the house in a sullen silence. Once again, I was five to ten feet behind her as we both made our way to the kitchen. The dishwasher needed to be unloaded. Wine needed to be opened and consumed.

Retreating to the family room, I pressed buttons on the TV remote, with a full glass of cabernet that ensured I'd not need to miss any of the final nine holes of the golf tournament I'd stumbled upon. *Yeah, I suppose that I was a member of the Fifty Percent men's club.* Then I dropped heavily into my favorite, brown-leather recliner, belt unbuckled (I'd enjoyed my Thai lunch), nonchalantly acting as if the conversation we'd had only moments before had never happened. I was hoping that she was doing the same. After all, I had simply conveyed to my wife of nearly nineteen years the feelings and observations that were bringing about my discontent with church, religion and—indirectly—my own life and sense of self. Discussing those feelings, doubts, and frustrations with my spouse was what I thought I was *supposed* to do. Honesty and open communication are two big skeleton keys that make a *good* marriage a *great* marriage. Or so I'd been told.

But the cease-fire was short-lived. It had also been a ruse. And I never expected what happened next.

As I sat comfortably nestled in my chair, my wife had quietly moved in from the kitchen, and now stood stoically beside the custom bookshelves we'd insisted upon having installed to display the many books we owned. My mind said, *don't look*. Instead, I looked in her direction. Glancing at her face, I sensed danger.

She stood with her body facing me, but her head was turned away, to the right. She was staring directly at the books which we'd purposely arranged in a designer-inspired, haphazard display of controlled chaos.

One bright, yellow book perched on the upper shelf captured her attention, one I'd purchased a few weeks earlier during one of my frequent trips to the local book store. *Buddhism for Dummies* had appealed to me for some reason as I'd scanned the shelves. I had never studied Buddhism and didn't know very much about it, but I was intrigued after reading the back cover.

I'd read the book during the daytime hours I'd spent alone at the house. It had been enlightening—no pun intended—and I felt a connection to something real and a sense of truth that that I'd never had in a lifetime spent within western mainstream religion.

Shit, meet fan.

"What the hell is *this*? So, are you a *Buddhist* now?"

That was her kneejerk reaction to merely *seeing* the book.

"No," I replied. "I've been reading about the philosophies of Buddhism. I think you'd like it. There are so many answers that . . ."

Apparently, 'I think you'd like it' weren't words she'd wanted to hear. Cutting me off mid-sentence and without hesitation, she reached to the right and forcefully yanked the book from the shelf. Then, raising the book above her head, she set her sights on me, and let it fly. This wasn't a smutty novel she'd discovered hidden there; she had thrown a book on one of the world's most peaceful spiritualities.

Somehow, I managed to avoid spilling my wine as I artfully dodged the missile intended for my head. It came at me like a Nolan Ryan spitball, hurled towards home plate for the last strikeout to win game seven of the World Series.

The spitball was followed by a barrage of comments of disbelief and disappointment.

"*So now you're not a Christian?*"

To a certain degree, she was scratching the surface of something that wasn't clear to me yet.

It was her turn to lead the conversation that I'd started earlier in the car. Now the conversation was different, but the theme was the same.

"You've been acting fucking weird for a while now, and I'm sick of it! First, you don't want to go to church with us! *Now* you're reading about Buddhism? What else are you reading? Are you studying Islam and plan to become a Muslim, too? Or maybe you wanna be Jewish? Is there a Torah on the shelf? Is this whole, 'I want to learn other religions thing' your bipolar disorder screwing with your thinking?"

I'd never mentioned that I had wanted to "learn other religions." Where did that come from?

Then, in mid-onslaught, the pattern that had emerged was suddenly crystal clear. Since that day when I'd been labeled as bipolar by her physician's assistant, she had been attributing any non-traditional way of thinking or any idiosyncrasy that she found odd or different to my "mental disorder". Once again, I saw that because I was not going along with the consensus reality, I was "ill".

Her reaction left no doubt that she'd also been aware of my increasing discontent with church, religion and, maybe, my own life and myself. She looked again to her right, scanning the books for other objectionable, blasphemous reading material.

She was confused, maybe frightened? Did she suddenly see writing on the wall?

I started to respond to her questions, trying to explain that in my search I was finding a huge chunk of vital information about 'God' and oneself that a lifetime of church sermons had never mentioned.

"I'm not Buddhist, or Jewish or anything else. I just feel...."

"You're wrong! Your feelings are wrong! You're not thinking clearly at all! It doesn't matter how you feel. Your feelings are wrong!"

Her words set me on fire. I may have found Hell—at that moment it was inside my whole diaphragm.

The implication that my feelings were just *wrong* was a punch, as well as a call to battle. Though we'd had our share of arguments throughout the years—as every couple does—for what may have been the first time in our marriage I considered her words to be a personal assault—a statement that belittled my worthiness as a person and an equal. I reacted with a strength of conviction that I'd never felt—a strength that came naturally and from a place deep within.

And it felt very, very good.

"What the *hell* are you doing? You just threw a fucking book at me! No, I'm not a Buddhist, Jew, Muslim, Atheist, or Satanist. I'm *curious*. I'm *unsettled* and I have *questions*. I need to know that there is more to my life and myself than anything that any preacher, church, religion or employer (there was an unspoken double-meaning in that reference) has force fed me while telling me it was the one and only thing to eat. What's wrong with that? You *know* that I read a lot. There are billions of people out there, and not all of them are Christian. I'm looking for answers to a lot of questions that I've *always* had and no one in my world has ever addressed let alone answered. You should have questions of your own!"

Tense silence.

Of course, I'd never attest to having all the answers, but no one had the right to tell me that my feelings were *wrong*. There are always differences of opinion, but to say that someone's feelings are wrong is the ultimate in attempted thought-control—basically, what I'd experienced organized religion doing . . . in a so-called "loving" way.

Then I injected what I believed to be a bit of levity.

"You know, if you'd read some of this book, you'd see that you just lost it and let anger control your thoughts and actions. Buddha would have a lot to say to you right now, and I'm pretty sure that Jesus wouldn't like what you just did all that much either."

If looks could kill, I'd have been flayed, cooked, and served on a platter.

She glared, and I sat in my chair, looking squarely at my wife with confidence and a strangely pleasant sense of accomplishment.

The truth was, she was not the enemy. If I'd seen that, I would have spared us all a bunch of pain and turmoil to come.

In hindsight, there are few events that carry with them the realization that you are on the right path so clearly as having a book proclaiming peace and love thrown at you by your spouse after church on a Sunday afternoon. This is especially true when the book is thrown by someone who claims to follow the teachings of love and peace in another book.

Irony can be such a great signpost. And this event was that.

After being bombed by *Buddhism for Dummies*, I knew that a large part of me had gone AWOL.

The house, the cars, the "stuff" hadn't mattered as much to me as they had to my wife and to most other people. Sure, "things" were nice to have, and I seemingly had it all—the perfect family, house, car, and yet another promising career. But although it *appeared* as if I had everything, inside I knew that all we had materially amounted to little or nothing spiritually. That little fact had just been proven to me in a profound way.

When my wife had stormed out of the room, a piece of me felt . . . well, okay . . . smug. Nolan Ryan would have been proud. My sixth-grade gym coach, who taught dodge ball tactics, would have been proud. But deeper inside, my true self—my spiritual self—wasn't celebrating. There comes a moment when you have no choice but to be brutally honest with yourself and other people—even those closest to you—about who you are. That moment determines whether you're going to grow and change in spirit or remain stagnant and slowly die inside.

I'd just gone through that moment. And it felt like some profound shift had taken place. A declaration of independence. A first statement about who I was and where I wanted my life to go.

I did not know that my statement was also a declaration of war. Today was just beginning; it was far from over.

I'd broken further away from the outer reality of the world I was living in. And that had posed a threat and challenge.

6

NO-MAN'S LAND

THUS FAR, MY SPIRITUAL AWAKENING—because messy as it was, that *is* what it was—had been an irregular series of *'aha'* moments of clarity. Each one came with a stronger awareness that, in the world where I was living, I was alone in a no-man's land.

Religiosity, societal norms, people's inability to think for themselves and the misguided importance of the "he who dies with the most toys, wins" rule now made me literally queasy in my stomach. On the flip-side, I was starting to be able to appreciate and *feel* nature. I'd spend entire afternoons mowing a postage stamp size lawn just so I could be outdoors for as long as possible. I'd often sneak outside—day or night—to sit on the steps, watching and listening to the wind rustle the tree leaves. Thunderstorms beckoned me to stand barefoot in the front yard, hands raised in the driving rain. Butterflies and bees fluttered and buzzed around me—sights and sounds I'd grown to take for granted. There was an odd feeling of oneness with nature—a feeling I'd known in my childhood as a boy playing in the woods behind my house.

I was also starting to gain an understanding of the importance of discernment. Like a record with a scratch, in my head I'd replay my own words used in conversations or arguments over and over. *I should have just listened. I could have said that another way. So and so isn't ready for this conversation . . . be patient.*

I was becoming much more sensitive to injustices. For example, this was the case when it came to the increasingly thoughtless polluting of the earth. Something as small and seemingly insignificant as seeing a cigarette butt being tossed to the ground was upsetting enough to bring a lump to my throat.

Witnessing the blatant lack of empathy for human suffering consistently exhibited by so many in Big Business and government—one in the same, actually—in exchange for bigger profits and executive bonuses was as unsettling as recognizing religious hypocrisies. More than infuriating, I saw it more like a knife slicing through a lifeline—a physical disconnect that was affecting everyone, everywhere.

To be clear, not everyone in business or government lacks empathy just like not everyone who adheres to religious teachings is hypocritical. Yet, I was still discontent and uncomfortable but the changes so far had been manageable and relatively painless.

The flying book had missed its mark.

That was all about to change. There was another song farther down in the juke-box queue of my life's soundtrack. It now made its way to the top.

There's something to be said for divine timing . . .

"Want a refill?"
"Yes please."
"Cabernet or merlot?"
Cabernet. Always a big, bold, kickass Cabernet.

"Cab is fine, thank you."

As mentioned earlier, mixing Wellbutrin and alcohol together with a big life transition is not a winning recipe, even though the temporary escape from stress feels like a good thing. The fact is, it prevents you from facing issues head-on and dealing with them wisely. Beyond that, frankly, it blocks your own, true spiritual progress or at the very least slows that progress to a crawl.

And so, this sad little exchange had become an almost nightly exchange between me and my wife for months. There was no need for her to ask the questions; she already knew the answers. But it was almost our only "dialogue" when we were alone. The marital gears, like so much else in my life, had nearly ground to a complete halt.

It was a muggy evening in late June, and after pouring wine, we sat in the living room in a silence wide and deep as the Grand Canyon, as mellow R&B tunes on the stereo filled the empty space between us. She was perched on the sofa, flipping through paperwork and taking the occasional sip of chardonnay. I had melted into my leather recliner, with a glass in one hand and the stereo remote in the other.

The atmosphere in the room was not so much empty as it was tense. It was the same atmosphere that had been present since the day I'd nearly been beaned by *Buddhism for Dummies*. The physical distance between us didn't go unnoticed. We both knew that the dynamics of our relationship had changed back on that day.

Everything was changing, and the discomfort of that was as unpleasant as it was unspoken.

"Hey, can we listen to something besides Al Green?" I asked. I wanted to hear something with a little, 'Hell Yeah!' rock-n-roll thump.

"Why? This is relaxing. I like this. We can listen to some Michael Buble if you want."

Geez, can we please move past the Michael Buble and Harry Connick, Jr. thing?

"Um, nah . . . let's pep it up a bit."

Not knowing what other CDs our kids may have slipped into the rotation, I pressed the remote's 'shuffle' button. I liked the feeling of not knowing what song was going to play every time I pressed it. The moment of silence between songs always held a morsel of suspense.

Please, no nouveaux country music . . . no nouveaux country music . . . .

On this night, the silence between songs was the calm before the storm. The stereo had randomly chosen a song by band that was the antithesis of Michael Buble or Keith Urban. Though I'd never heard this tune, it began with the thumping vibe I was hoping for.

Perfect! A rock riff with a great beat and *a band that can play the instruments. No synth-pop, same 'ol, same 'ol. No Buble-esque crooning. No twangy, 'pop-goes-the-country' Charlie Daniels wannabe. Ah, just what I was wanting . . . .*

Apparently, I was alone in my appreciation of the stereo's "random" song selection.

"Jeff! Where'd you find this crap? Play something else."

Setting her paperwork aside, my wife stood, turned and headed in my direction. Grabbing the remote from my hand, she began pressing one button after another with a focused effort to change the song.

"How do you change the damned song?"

The song had captured my attention with the first line in the lyrics. Her question fell on deaf ears.

"Listen to this . . . damn, this song is talking to us! Listen! It hits home, don't you think?"

It's punching me like a boxer works a speed bag, and I'm the speed bag.

"It's not talking to me. It's crap. It's filthy! How do you change the CD?"

Your discernment was taking a break. It wasn't "talking to her."

"Hold on, I really like this. Just let me listen."

The song was just beginning to fade out when she finally found the elusive 'shuffle' button.

"There, that's better. Michael Buble—*good* music. Nice and smooth."

Nice and smooth. Calming and refined. Domesticated... settled ... conformed. Damn. I am a Michael Buble album.

I never found out how the other CD made it into the rotation or where it came from. My kids claimed they'd never heard the song or the band and that the CD wasn't one of theirs. Yet, the disk was in the stereo and the song was in the queue. I would come to understand that there are no coincidences and stranger things than this happen.

The song that was inadvertently added to my life's soundtrack—the spork in our road—the song that sent my journey into warp speed was *"Fake It"* –by the Australian band, Seether:

> *Who's to know if your soul will fade at all*
> *The one you sold to fool the world*
> *You lost your self-esteem along the way*
> *Good God you're coming up with reasons*
> *Good God you're dragging it out*
> *Good God it's the changing of the seasons*
> *I feel so raped*
> *So follow me down*
> *And just fake it if you're out of direction*

Fake it, if you don't belong here
Fake it, if you feel like infection
Woah you're such a fucking hypocrite
And who's to know that the lies won't hide your flaws
No sense in hiding all of yours
You gave up on your dreams along the way
And just fake it if you're out of direction
Fake it, if you don't belong here
Fake it, if you feel like infection
Woah you're such a fucking hypocrite
I can fake with the best of anyone
I can fake with the best of 'em all
I can fake with the best of anyone
I can fake it all . . . .

 It had taken roughly four minutes—the length of that one song—for me to become aware that I was alone on an unfamiliar road leading to god-knows-where.
 I looked across at my wife, and the chasm seemed wider. She was continuing onward, now facing the opposite direction from where I was headed—*where I wanted to head!*—and she was also alone on a road we'd traveled together moments earlier.
 The thing was, we had both listened to the lyrics. I knew she'd heard them, and that her desperation to silence them was a painful attempt to keep the truth from smashing the life we'd built to this point. The message, however, was blatantly obvious. I *knew* that she'd received it; that was visible in the expression on her face and the frustration in her words

 I had recognized, received and whole-heartedly embraced the message in the lyrics. It was a gut-check that carried with it an acknowledgement of imperfection. I stood alone in that acknowledgement of imperfection. I had been "faking it" in some fashion most of my lifetime. I was a human being with human qualities. No trendy clothing makeover or teeth whitening changed the fact that I was short, enjoyed wine to excess, tried like hell to be someone—anyone—other than who I truly was. The list was long and we all have our own list of imperfections. It's difficult to come face to face with a truth that exposes yourself. It's even more difficult to accept that truth. Acceptance requires change. Change can be an amazingly beautiful thing: change can also unleash a mother-load of pain.

In your case, a mother-load with a capital "M" and capital "L".

We knew it; we couldn't say it.
We had been faking it as a couple for a long, long time.
One of us could not tolerate that life any longer.

THE CHAOS ZONE

IN HIS AMAZING BOOK, *Myths to Live By*, Joseph Campbell talks about the soul's journey as one in which we set out to find and regather pieces of our true self that have been broken off and are missing from our awareness. He addressed the fact that people have often used various substances—drugs, alcohol—to try to induce the journey out of one level of consciousness to another, trying to find the missing piece or pieces. This, he says, has its costs.

". . . one breaks away from the world, plunging inward, and ranges of vision are experienced and are in fact the same as those of a psychosis. But what, then, is the difference? What is the difference between a psychotic or LSD experience and a yogic, or a mystical? The plunges are all into the same deep inward sea; of that there can be no doubt. The symbolic figures encountered are in many instances identical [. . .]. But there is an important difference. The difference—to put it sharply—is equivalent simply to that between a diver who can swim and one who cannot. The mystic, endowed with native talents for this sort of thing and following, stage by stage, the instruction of a master, enters the waters and finds he can swim; whereas the schizophrenic, unprepared, unguided, and ungifted, has fallen or has intentionally plunged, and is drowning."

That was you. As always, blindly jumping in feet first . . . trial by fire.

Because I had no clue what was really happening to me, and because I had no guidance or instruction about the soul's true journey—well, I wasn't drowning, but I was seriously floundering in what felt like a huge ocean. And if drinking and taking anti-depressants to escape the craziness of that wasn't bad enough, I took a step toward making life better that would first make life a whole lot worse.

"Hey man . . . you have a death wish," my next-door neighbor once told me.

If I'd heard it once, I'd heard it a thousand times.

"Dude, you got a death wish or somethin'?" a couple of Navy Seals once asked me.

Damn, Jeff . . . you reached between two Navy Seals and brazenly grabbed fries from their plates. Either of them could have killed you with a pinkie finger. It's a good thing you have a sense of humor and made them laugh. There must be a reason that you're still alive and kickin'.

In response to the Seals and to my neighbor, the response was the same.

"Yeah, I sure do."

I don't recall exactly what I'd said or done to prompt that

observation from my neighbor, though I do remember the look of wariness on his face. I felt like a man who had betrayed his tribe to join another. The truth was, I was in no man's land, wishing I knew where the hell I was headed. I only knew I liked the new, kind of reckless feeling that was starting to drive me forward.

When my soul sucker-punched me and said, *Hey! It's time to be authentic! Ditch the old persona and embrace your true nature*—it did so with authority. When I looked at myself in the mirror, I couldn't believe who I'd become. I had been the proverbial frog in a slowly-heated pot of water, and I was disgusted, and ready to shed the things that marked me as belonging to the tribe of the American "upper-middle-and-climbing class".

The person looking back at me in the mirror was a creation— not unlike Frankenstein's monster. However, I admit that I looked good. I was in great shape. My hair was coiffed—a nod to the professional stylist who was also a trainer for Rusk hair care products. My teeth—likely visible from space—were whitened to brilliant perfection. They were the complement to my deeply-bronzed skin—tanning had become my therapy. Yet, that wasn't me.

Why am I wearing mock turtlenecks and tapered slacks? I'm a freakin' metro sexual! What happened to my ball caps and rock band t-shirts? Who the hell is that guy? I don't recognize him. How'd he get here? When did he get here?

Now, I couldn't shake the song "Fake It" from my head.

And who's to know that the lies won't hide your flaws
No sense in hiding all of yours
You gave up on your dreams along the way.

I had acquaintances, no real "tribe" of my own. I was *accepted* by my wife's 'friends'—the ones who played the game for their own career advancement. For several years now I'd played the role of 'corporate spouse' very well, going as far as altering my voice so my southern accent wasn't as noticeable to potential employers and 'sophisticated' people.

At least the rift between us was changing that, making it easier for me to separate myself a little from that world. At some point, she stopped introducing me to her colleagues during corporate functions. The first time it happened was disheartening. There wasn't a second time—I rectified her omission by introducing myself. "Hello! Nice to meet you! I'm Jeff. I live with her and I can iron bedsheets with unrivaled perfection."

I'd gotten "the look."

One too many times.

Remember, I mentioned taking a step that would first make things worse? Buckle up.

It was on a chilly October evening that the main threads that had held together my old life ripped apart at the seams.

We were attending a party for the couple who lived across the street. They had married earlier that day and invited the entire neighborhood to an outdoor reception. We'd been there maybe thirty minutes when I noticed my wife making the rounds, telling everyone that we had to leave.

"Goodnight, y'all . . . Sorry to leave so early, but we have to get up early for church," she said with a smile.

By this time, I'd stopped attending church, though. So, why the pretense that *we* were going? I also knew that *she* wasn't even planning on going to church the next day.

And so, when I heard her excuse for leaving, there was a little *click* within me.

Good God you're coming up with reasons
Good God you're dragging it out
Good God it's the changing of the seasons
I feel so raped
So follow me down. . . .

"You go ahead," I commented. "I'm gonna hang out for a while."

My words were met with a smile, but underneath I saw the all too familiar anger.

"Don't be too long."

Uh huh . . . okey-dokey.

That moment wasn't the beginning of the end of my marriage; that moment had come months earlier. Fifteen minutes later, I gave it the inevitable sword thrust.

In hindsight, it was a destructive act.

Having distanced myself from the crowd, I was drinking a beer and talking with a couple of the neighbors about sports or work—topics I had *never* enjoyed discussing—when, without hesitation, I blurted out, "Hey, I met this woman online. She's beautiful, smart, funny, and most of all she really gets and appreciates me for who I am."

Yeah, you said it.

The men just stood there listening, smiling, and nodding in silence. I wasn't inebriated, I was confident and—to be quite honest—wasn't inhibited by potential backlash.

You could have stopped there, Jeff. But no, that wasn't an option.

"It's crazy! Believe it or not, we met on an adult website—yeah, one of those 'discreet' sites—and, get this, the first time that we met, we both knew there was something strong between us. We sat under a tree at a winery, drank wine, ate cheese, and talked for five straight hours."

The head nods and awkward smiles continued, but no one said a word. I had crossed some sort of man-to-man confidentiality line and opened Pandora's Box, but I didn't care. The words kept coming. I had wanted to share this news with the world.
"She's married, but her husband is cool with it. Hell, he even 'interviewed' me before she and I ever, you know, got together—*wink, wink.*"
My enthusiasm was now met with stiff, forced smiles. One of the guys backed away a step or two as he listened.

There are no take-backs, Jeff. You're the one who put it out there. Time to face that music.

My enthusiastic revelation didn't take long to make its way across the street to my wife's ears.
I returned to the house less than an hour after I'd dropped that bombshell. I'd opted to stay downstairs for a short while, not aware that the news had traveled so quickly.
With the stealth of a ninja, my wife appeared. The moment was rather embarrassing and quite startling—given the fact that I was in the bathroom, texting the woman I'd moments ago been discussing with the neighbors.

And just fake it if you're out of direction
Fake it, if you don't belong here
Fake it, if you feel like infection
You're such a fucking hypocrite . . . .

Not anymore.

"Yes," I answered her angry question. "Yes, I have met someone new."

Was I an idiot that night, for just blurting out the truth instead of pretending we were still the nice, church-going couple? Most might say, yes. It was an impulsive act, to cut through the bullshit even I had held in place far too long.

Should I have left one relationship before starting another? That would have made things cleaner, for damn sure. That's the societal protocol, after all.

Do I feel remorse for the pain I brought to my wife and kids? *Absolutely, I do.*

Do I regret meeting another woman—in particular, *this* amazing woman—while I was still married? *No—a million times, no.* But that's because there is a whole lot more to that story, which I will get to later.

It's a bit difficult when I look back to that evening. Until then, songs had spoken truths through lyrics. That night, an energy that was driving me—no, not lust—caused me to say the truth, *I can no longer live halfway between one world and another. Life doesn't come with a rule book.*

What that other world was, I didn't know, though its bright outlines were starting to appear and become increasingly clear with each passing day.

My wife and I didn't immediately go our separate ways after that night. The spiritual war—old self *versus* authentic, emerging self—would eventually require my departure, but during that messy time the casualties would rapidly accumulate. The sense of an unseen and greater reality was still there, beckoning and shining vividly, and yet of course I was very much in this solid world of things. This chaotic sense of two realities side by side made the life transition an uneven ground to cross.

One of the earlier casualties during this time was my career. More precisely, I chose to say, "*No, thank you*," to all of life's little luxuries I'd enjoyed for so many years. The custom-built house with my own 'man cave' office—a house in which I'd never felt at home—was now just another house. The ungodly number of designer clothes—many with tags still attached—hanging in the closet and played a part in defining me in the eyes of the world I now looked at as needless excess that caused me to feel ashamed.

Why did you want so much stuff, Jeff? You were the guy from a small town, who never chased money or possessions.

Now at least I knew for sure I didn't *need* all the 'stuff.' Not once had the clothes, gadgets, trips—the highlighted hair- or other things that money provided ever given me more than temporary happiness. I had *wanted* the 'stuff.' I didn't need the excesses. I hadn't known what it was that I needed. The 'stuff' had filled a void, much like alcohol, sex, drugs, sex, or television.

Yes, I purposely mentioned sex twice. Three times would be too obvious.

Thankfully, I wasn't without a job, technically speaking.

A few months earlier, I had left my job as North American Sales Manager for an overseas company in order to be at the house when the kids arrived from school, made possible by my wife's income. Now, in addition to selling unworn designer clothes on eBay, I had taken a job walking dogs for a small pet-sitting service.

Yes, I transitioned from a white-collar career to a dog collar job.

I sold every business suit I owned, severed my connections to the white-collar world and swore to never again play the role of 'aspiring business executive.' It was the most liberating feeling I'd had in more than twenty years of employment. And there was a hint of giddiness in my voice when I said "yes" to the part-time job walking dogs. Shorts, sneakers and t-shirts replaced creased slacks, starched shirts and wingtips. Bending over to bag up dog poop replaced, well, just bending over, if you get my drift. I walked dogs in pouring rain, cold snow and scorching heat. And, I absolutely loved doing it.

Though it hadn't ended up being my childhood dream job of an astronaut orbiting the earth—what I considered to be ultimate freedom—walking dogs and feeding cats was the polar opposite of what I'd been doing: managing the national sales of blast protection equipment to government and military agencies. The dogs were always overjoyed to see me when I arrived. Not once do I remember a government employee being overjoyed when I'd walk through the door, briefcase in hand.

Crazy at it sounds when you've lived in the tribe of the upper-middle-income class, when you've accepted that consensus reality, the path of simple joy made me feel something I hadn't felt in a long time.

Joy.

I felt alive being outdoors, and I felt appreciated by the company's owner. And, I so enjoyed the job that being paid the small amount of $5.50 per walk seemed unfair—not unfair to me but unfair to the young guy who owned the pet service. The only downside—seven walks a day, five days a week and, well, you can do the math. The job certainly didn't provide the income or help support the lifestyle to which I'd been so accustomed. I didn't care. I somehow felt—*knew*—that everything was going to be okay. It was the same feeling—*knowing*—I'd felt at other times of uncertainty.

My life was being flipped upside-down, yet my spirit and sense of self was stronger than it had been in many years. The transition I'd hungered for was taking place. Not in a way I would have planned or expected, but it was happening, and I felt a kind of growing excitement.

And you haven't even gotten to the bizarrely interesting parts yet.

I've mentioned that things got messy. Well, they did. I am aware that not everyone who goes through a spiritual transition like mine—from an orientation to solid-world realities to unseen-world realties—goes through the turmoil I did. Mine was more upheaval than transition. An upheaval is not a requirement. In some ways, maybe I was giving the world I'd lived in a smack in the face as I gave it the heave-ho, and that caused some of the messiness. And not everyone pays as big a cost. That's not a requirement either.

Soon after my wife and I finally separated (I had moved out and returned to the house one time), I purchased the pet service with much of the money received as a part of our separation agreement. In return, I conceded nearly everything, including my portion of ownership in the house, my rights to a portion of her retirement account, all my collectible sports memorabilia and my five-burner gas grill. I did, however, take sheets and a couple of towels.

You really thought that out, didn't ya, Jeff?

I would own that pet service for eight years before giving it to one of my employees—a wonderful person who had been through hell and finally left behind an old life to really *live* . . . just as I had done. That little pet service sustained me financially, though, at a time when I needed it most.

Throughout the chaos of those months, virtually everything that happened was attributed to my *supposed* Bipolar Disorder. Infidelity, multiple arrests, moving from the house to an apartment then back again to the house, a few hospitalizations—all were attributed to my 'suffering' from Bipolar Disorder.

"You're highly manic," I was told.

Never once prior to that time had my sanity come into question. Suddenly, I was "highly manic"—a condition of Bipolar Disorder that lasts a few weeks, at most—whenever I did or said anything that wasn't considered normal. If indeed I'd been highly manic, I'd been that way for roughly seven months or longer surely setting a record worthy of mention in some mental health trade journal and the DSM.

Huh. You must have been an anomaly or an enigma . . . or both.

At one point, at the insistence of the court after a short vacation in the county detention center, I underwent psychological testing. After more than six consecutive hours of tests and evaluations, three psychiatrists and two test administrators had grouped together and were whispering. None could formulate an explanation for what I'd begun to experience.

Hang on, here it comes. Here's where they say, "No way."

For instance, when I was outside I had begun to see natural objects and phenomena—trees, wind, stones—composed of a random series of 5s, 8s, 3s, and other digits.

When this first occurred, it startled me—but almost immediately, I realized that everything is built on mathematical structures. The nautilus shell, for instance, and many other natural objects, grow in what is known as "the golden mean", a certain sequence of increasing spaces that create a perfect and expanding spiral form. Even the form of objects that are exploding can be "described" by extremely complex numerical equations.

Is that what I was suddenly seeing—the mathematics behind created things? Albert Einstein had envisioned the invisible quantum world when he realized his theory of relativity, and spoke of the equation $E=mc^2$ as seeing part of "the mind of God."

There were more changes. I had begun to see each day painted a color, as if I were seeing it through a tinted lens. A day had a certain feel that corresponded with that color. Most often, a day's color was tinted yellow, green, or blue. Occasionally, I'd have a day overcast in red. Red days were never good days. Thankfully, the red days were few and far between.

Most interesting, at least to me, the think-tank of specialists was stymied and unwilling to even attempt an explanation, as to why I had a sudden knowledge of quantum mechanics. Never had I studied physics. My exposure to formal science ended with high school biology.

What would any highly-trained psychiatrist do in this case? Of course, they would alter medications—again—and slap a label on my chest: "Hi, My Name is _____ and I Am Highly Manic. *Warning!*"

Elevated by this new energy that was driving me—well, ironically, I was about to hit some new lows.

I had packed a bag, intending to leave the house during a difficult time, when my wife stepped surely in my path as I moved towards the bedroom door, blocking my exit. I wasn't aware that my wife had moments earlier phoned the police, insisting that I was in no condition to drive or be in public. I wasn't impaired by alcohol or any other substance, I only wished to leave. But in her mind I suffered from Bipolar Disorder and might hurt myself.

According to the Public Defender in the Commonwealth of Virginia, tapping someone on the shoulder without approval is a crime. That night, I had taken my wife's arms and moved her to the side. There was no violence—no shove, no push, *nothing*. But when the police arrived, they asked if I'd touched her. Without knowing that I'd be arrested, my wife said, "Yes, he just moved me from the doorway."

Hands behind your back, Jeff, you're going for a ride. Well, I'll be a son of a . . .

Without missing a beat, they handcuffed and escorted me from the house, as I quipped, trying to bring some levity to the bizarre moment, "Hey, that's a nice gun—red-tipped or real? Can I hold it a sec?"

One of the officers looked startled, and the other chuckled. All of this happened as my wife, kids and her parents watched in silence.

At 1:30 A.M. I was released from the county jail. I'd been told I wasn't to contact my wife, not even by smoke signal, for seventy-two hours. The restraining order wasn't even put in place by my wife. "Virginia is for Lovers" is the state motto. More irony.

When the door was opened and I was given the green light to exit, I had nowhere to go and no way to get anywhere.

"Can I get a ride somewhere?" I'd assumed that one of the

hundreds of officers at the county lockup could at least drop me off at a Hampton Inn. Protect *and* Serve, right?

Nope.

So, on a snowy, late January morning, I walked five miles, without a jacket, towards the only place I could think to go. My house. After walking a mile or so in the cold darkness, I used my cell phone and called the house, asking my wife to call a taxi. *Big no-no*. Arrest number two happened the next morning, for violating the restraining order.

As an important side-note, no one over the course of those few days—not the officers who arrested me, the officers at the jail, the medical examiner at the detention center, the judge who set me free on bail, or the public defender—not a single person recognized behavior symptomatic of someone with Bipolar Disorder. Even though I'd been slapped with that diagnosis for several years.

The lyrics to *'It's My Life'* kept coming to mind during that time, even as I was lying on a paper-thin mattress on the floor of a jail cell—curled in the fetal position, facing the wall with my head under a toilet (two to a cell, only one bunk).

> *This ain't a song for the broken-hearted*
> *No silent prayer for the faith-departed*
> *I ain't gonna be just a face in the crowd*
> *You're gonna hear my voice*
> *When I shout it out loud.*

The inmate I bunked with had stabbed someone. After talking with him, under his gruff persona he was a good guy, just misdirected and scared. He wished me well when I was released.

Why am I sharing all this in detail?

I went through a full frontal nuclear assault in those seven months. There were aftershocks for months afterwards. I lost everything. My identity, the material 'stuff', my marriage, my kids—everything I'd believed was true—all swept away by wave after wave of increased *self-awareness* and by a rapidly growing awareness that *a reality exists beyond the one we can see, taste, smell, and touch.*

I also share this chaotic transition because of a truth I later realized: Everything that happened during that time was the result of my having *chosen* to live a life that wasn't authentic. Those things also happened because of my choices—words and actions—during that time.

Despite inwardly knowing that it wasn't *my* life, the perks that came with that life had multiplied like rabbits. My distaste for materialism and increasing frustration at the thought of my life having no real meaning seemed to quietly step aside when those perks arrived.

Or, maybe you pushed them aside.

To be sure, there were days I could have kicked myself. I sometimes thought back to the day when I stared from the bedroom window and considered myself an 'employee'—a non-entity—without sense of self or purpose. Why didn't I stay in that comfortable, prescribed pattern?

You knew why, even then. It was a coffin. And you had a calling no one knew how to identify, much less train you for.

As a result, there were many mornings I'd stand in front of the bathroom mirror frozen in place, a blank stare on my face, lost.

There were nights I'd pull the sheets to my chin before drifting off to sleep, thinking, *Please, don't let me wake up . . . I can't do this anymore.*

On those nights, I resigned myself to the belief that *my life* was for the most part, gone.

I have *never* been so grateful for being so wrong. What I had to endure—to survive—to liberate my soul, I wouldn't wish on my worst enemy. Then again, I would soon realize that I had no "enemies". Not anymore.

As Jimmy Buffett would say,

> *I'm growing older but not up*
> *My metabolic rate is pleasantly stuck*
> *So let the winds of change blow over my head*
> *I'd rather die while I'm living than live while I'm dead.*
> *. . . . I'd rather die while I'm living than live while I'm dead . . . .*

So much was lying ahead awaiting my arrival. I had given up or lost every *thing* . . . and I was about to gain *everything*.

8

THE POWER

BACK TO PAMELA.

Alright, here's the lowdown on the messiest aspect of my transition, the part that ain't pretty by conventional standards. Some might even say it was reprehensible. So be it. As a very special someone would later tell me, *"It is what it is."* I'll not mince words. Yes, I began a new relationship before I ended my marriage. Before casting me into Hell, a place I'm quite adept at navigating on my own, hear me out.

Long before meeting my wife, I had unknowingly embarked on a soul journey in search of an elusive *something* that was painfully missing from my life. I didn't even know that I was on a search.

Now, always up for an adventure, I had cranked up it up a few notches, and dove into a "discrete" online "search". I'd been in the mode of constant dissatisfaction after all, and selfishly that was all I was thinking about at the time.

What the hell—right? What could it hurt? No, don't answer that . . .

I actually belly-flopped into the internet's sordid side of the dating pool. I didn't visit the traditional dating sites. I visited and subsequently became a member of only one site—an adult 'hookup' site—AdultFriendFinder.com. Many members were men, most likely married men. Lonely women, married women, wild women, adventurous couples, bisexuals, gay men and women, and at least one person from nearly every lifestyle were present and accounted for on AFF. I had stumbled upon a smorgasbord of illicitness and, damn, I was intrigued and titillated.

C'mon, I had to use 'titillated' in the description.

Ironically, when I wasn't being repulsed by *'crotch shots'* and *'dick pics'* while browsing the profiles, I was spending most of my time on the website writing. The site featured a blog section for members and my blog somehow appealed to quite a few members. To my credit, I never denied being a married man. I wrote about my frustrations, observations, things I couldn't or wouldn't say to my wife. Every post was humorous, whether it was a rant or an off-the-cuff, fictional sex romp. Other times, I merely chatted with other members.

I made a few friends who *weren't* perverts or cheaters. Despite the thrill and the prospect of meeting someone for a casual, untamed sexual experience—several opportunities presented themselves—I couldn't bring myself to follow through. It wasn't the guilt of knowing that I was stepping, albeit only slightly, outside of my marriage that prevented me from engaging in a casual roll in the hay. The opportunities were tempting but the vibes weren't there.

It just never felt right.

No one had whatever it was that would make the encounter worth pursuing. I just had a *knowing* that no one I could have hooked up with had 'it'—whatever 'it' might have been. Casual, meaningless sex wasn't what I needed or wanted.

Are you crazy? Isn't that what the site is intended to provide? Isn't that why guys go to sites like those? Call me quirky. I've always said that not all guys think the same way.

Remember, my wife and I had started to split apart long before we separated and I moved from the house—and all during that time I was growing disenchanted and intensely frustrated with us and with our situation. I was far more detached from my old self and my old life than I knew, probably because I was still physically in my old environment, while my mind and soul were already out the door. In the back of my mind, I was dabbling at playing "what if. . . ?"

During that time, out of nowhere, I stumbled upon something unexpected—or rather *someone* who would change me, redirect my life, and aim a blowtorch at the candle of my own, flickering spirituality.

She was beautiful—a magnificently beautiful butterfly.

Pamela's profile photo was strikingly artistic. She was standing outside with her back to the camera—long, flowing red hair contrasting magnificently against alabaster skin. She was wearing a white mask, made barely visible by a slight, upward tilt of her head. A simple white skirt covered her lower body, and her arms reached upwards towards the sky. Her pose was graceful, elegant, and reminiscent of a butterfly.

It was a moment, and a *knowing* I would never forget.

I'd found the photo while browsing the "couples seeking couples" section of the site. I had no intention of contacting her—or them—for any reason other than to comment on the profile photo, which is what I did. I was compelled to share my admiration. I felt I had no choice but to compose a short message, complimenting the choice of profile picture.

"*Beautiful photo! Thank you for choosing to show that beauty and grace exists in a world of vulgarity. Are you sure you're in the right place?*"

I clicked "Send", and resumed browsing, not giving any thought to the possibility of receiving a reply message. I had only wanted to say, "*Thank you.*"

Less than two weeks later, *everything* changed in the amount of time it takes to open an email.

Come on, you jumped the curb, went off-road and started doing donuts. "Eat my dust!"

Here's a truth about the spiritual journey, one that may only make sense when you've lived it and it has walked you out of the consensus reality agreed upon by society at large. I'm talking about rules, and how we live in relation to them. Some are good, others are meant to bend, and others to be broken. And then, there are rules that are perceptions—societal mindsets and beliefs—that do not universally apply to everyone.

I threw the rulebook written by social perception out the window. That didn't relieve me from experiencing the karmic ramifications of breaking those perceived societal rules, but it did lead me to places—and people—I'd never have known had I not tossed the rulebook.

Men create the rules. The soul creates the men.

It was just *another day in paradise.*

Let's see if there's anything new happening out there in lonely land, I thought, opening my email at AdultFriendFinder.com. I'd posted a blog entry on my profile page, but didn't have much of a response to it.

What spam do I have today? Should I just bite the bullet, and buy those penis enlargement pills and *the 'guaranteed to work' pheromones?*

I opened the inbox and noticed a message titled, *Re: Beautiful profile photo!*

I knew that it was from the redhead that caught my eye a couple of weeks earlier. I hadn't sent anyone other than her an email with that title. Her picture was unlike any other on the site.

I opened the email fully expecting the standard, 'Thanks, but no thanks,' response. After reading her reply I'm pretty sure that I raised my arms and loudly exclaimed, *You've gotta be kidding me!* I was in two states at once—disbelief and jubilance.

Oddly enough, it was a married man who had stumbled upon my blog entry. He happened to be the *husband* of the redhead beauty. It was he who had read the blog, which I'd titled *Vacation from Hell,* describing a recent getaway with in-laws, and enjoyed the humor in my tale of suffering. As a result, he'd asked her to read it. Putting two and two together, they determined that my story and the complimentary email were both penned by the same guy. In an act of adult website defiance, they threw caution—and the "Couples Seeking Couples" rulebook—out the window.

With the husband's blessing, the woman I'd compared to a butterfly replied to my message. At that moment, many lives—mine, hers, our family members, friends, the dry cleaner, *etc.*—ventured off into new directions.

Even I sometimes have a hard time believing all that transpired on this leg of the journey, which took me outside the "rules". If I hadn't lived it, there's no way I'd believe all that happened and if I were to include everything that transpired, it would take three volumes. But this part did happen, and without it, my journey may have come to a tragic, premature ending.

Pamela—the woman I'd later speak about during a neighborhood gathering—and I were soon having lengthy conversations both by phone and instant message. She and her husband were also in a transition phase of their marriage, though they were being more honest and open about it than my wife and I could be, because of the religious boundaries we were trying to live within. Pamela also sent additional photos of herself in her reply message. My jaw dropped. Every photo was as tasteful as the first.

My god, she's gorgeous!

A quick self-check told me she was out of my league. Yet something prodded and nudged me to forge ahead. Within a week, for the first and only time since I'd been a member of the site, I gathered the nerve and asked to meet. I was both thrilled and petrified when she agreed without hesitation. I was aware that what I was doing wasn't considered acceptable behavior for a married man.

Each time I'd thought about the possibility of meeting someone on the site, a small voice had whispered, *This isn't right, you're a married man.* Yet, this time, there was no whisper. There was more than simple physical attraction—there was a magnetism, a connection, unlike anything I'd experienced. It *felt* right. I was *compelled* to meet this woman.

We chose to meet on a Wednesday, in a public place. A winery—go figure—for the sole purpose of getting better acquainted. I experienced a massive wave of nervous euphoria from the moment I first laid eyes upon her. As she climbed from her car, I felt a surge of emotion. Excitement, relief, nervousness—joy—were intermingled. So intense was the emotion that I nearly forgot to hand her the bouquet of sunflowers that I'd purchased for the occasion.

Whereas I experienced *joy* when I left my old career path, I instantly experienced something completely new and life-giving the instant I met Pamela—a force that drew me in, and opened me up in a way I'd never known, at least not that I was yet aware.

To begin with, though I'd dated quite a few women in my lifetime and was married, none exuded the warmth and genuineness that radiated from Pamela—and there was something else.

A transformational moment was occurring.

David Hawkins, who I mentioned earlier, says in his book, *Power Vs. Force*, "Love is misunderstood to be an emotion; actually, it is a state of awareness, a way of being in the world, a way of seeing oneself and others." Hawkins, a physicist, is also known for having measured the energy levels of different states of being. *Depression* has very low energy level, and slightly up the scale are *fear* and *anger*—each holding more energy, though not necessarily good energy states to be in. At the top of the human energy scale, exponentially higher than all others, is the energy of love—an energy great enough to cause mental, spiritual, and even physical healing.

Whereas I'd lived for decades merely existing at low-energy levels—fearing judgment and criticism, depressing my own personal desires believing I was doing the right thing, serving the right belief system, angry at others who seemed to be to blame for my unhappiness and angry at myself for not feeling powerful enough to do something about my life—I now, suddenly encountered a force that blew me sky-high. I'd experienced a small dose of it, seeing Pamela's pictures and talking with her on the phone. Now I was encountered a living, breathing, full-measure dose.

I found myself in the presence of a pure, selfless *love*.

We're talkin' spiritual plutonium. Heavenly Hazmat.

We purchased a couple bottles of wine and settled outdoors on a blanket between two large trees. Even as this rare and beautiful energy surrounded and engulfed us, we were both nervous as we nibbled on various cheeses and popped the cork on a bottle of cabernet. We were engulfed, too, in a timeless space, and for five hours we sat engaged in conversation.

It was as if we rode on a current of pure energy, sharing our movement away from organized religion, thoughts on spirituality, numerology, love, marriage, children. Although it wasn't obvious at the time, we were both searching for the same thing—the true path our lives should be on.

There wasn't much talk of a sexual nature. Instead, the conversation provided us with insights into aspects of ourselves and each other. We realized we were both creations of the unrealistic expectations placed upon us by religion, families, society, and the world in general. We were kindred spirits—a sense that we'd both later admit having even prior to that day, when we'd first connected online. She was not only a soulmate—a widely misunderstood word—she was much more. She was part of me, the Yin to my Yang, my twin flame.

It was if we'd known each other for our entire lifetimes. Yes, *lifetimes*. I knew exactly what I was doing. I knew that it wasn't kosher. Yet, didn't feel a shred of guilt. This felt different somehow. The connection between us was a visible, palpable, undeniable energy.

I felt *alive*. I felt *needed*. I felt as if I'd entered another realm—a state defined by perfect acceptance just exactly the way I was, without having to cover up, without having to compete or achieve status. I felt as if I were starting to heal from a deep, deep soul wound I'd never known I'd had until that moment. And everything about this encounter—meeting out of bounds, our intense connection—felt strangely and perfectly *right*.

It was all a little bit mind blowing. Yet, I'd never felt such surety and confidence in my life. The path I needed to be on ran in this direction—toward pure love.

As you now know, the five hours I'd spent with Pamela at the winery ignited a firestorm of chaotic, forbidden and mind-numbing events—both good and bad. It was if I had slicked my hair into a ducktail, donned a zippered, leather jacket and thrown my leg over a black Harley-Davidson chopper. I rode fast and hard with no helmet but I began to gain greater clarity as I spent more of my time with Pamela. I was not wise enough to avoid the stage of transition that I now refer to as the 'rebel *with* a cause.' Lacking in wisdom, I acted in ways that brought harm to others and to myself, actions I will forever regret.

Still, the course was set, and at a very deep level I now felt sure of it—I had to follow the path this newly-encountered energy called me to. What had been a sensing, then a whisper, then a voice, had now become an embodied power coursing through me.

The only nervousness I felt occurred during my 'interview.' Pamela's husband had asked that I meet with both together and undergo an interview of sorts before our relationship progressed. Apparently, I passed the interview. I'll leave it at that.

Back to my marriage, briefly. Eventually, there was a moment that brought the 'will you stay or will you go?' discussions to a halt. My wife asked, "Do you love her?"

Without hesitation, I replied, "*Yes, yes I do.*"

I'd never been so sure of something in my entire life. I had not hesitated to reply. I surprised myself with the ease in which I gave my response. I loved the fact that I could be open about the unusual experiences I was having, and not be judged or censored but accepted. I loved the state of being that openness and spiritual exploration allowed Pamela and me to enter into when we were together.

When we were together, we were in a world without walls. Anything was possible.

In that moment I professed my love for Pamela, of course, I closed the door on one life and began another. My children—then seventeen and twelve—were surely confused, but remained open to spending time with me, at least for a while. Within a few weeks, they abruptly ended all communication with me. Honestly, I don't blame *them*. I suppose I wasn't the model father and typical *cul-de-sac* Dad. Then again, I had never fit that mold. But, during that time, my life was in full upheaval mode.

That moment in time carried with it a whirlwind of emotion and massive change.

I left my house, my cache of toys, material comfort and financial security—not to mention a family and extended family—sure of only one thing: I had found the head of my path. I was free of pretending to be someone other than myself, though I hadn't yet put all the pieces to that puzzle together. I wasn't clear about where I would be going or what life had in store for me but I felt a sense of peace and that unexplainable *knowing* that everything would be okay—that I would be alright. I had brazenly taken a step towards reclaiming my authentic self. Everything that had happened along the way—the numerous moments that had opened my eyes a bit more—had led to this.

As I gained in a new more potent awareness of the world and myself, my senses were dramatically heightened. I felt liberated—free to be myself.

Looking back, although I didn't feel guilty about what I'd done or why I'd stepped into another realm at that time in my life,

I did feel remorse for the way I handled some of the events of that time. It wasn't until a few years later that only self-forgiveness could extinguish those flames of remorse.

9

EYES AND EARS OPEN

AFTER MY SEPARATION, I lived on my own in an apartment. It was a tumultuous time of consequences for some unwise behavior in the face of the "norms", but also a time when the awakening continued. Eventually, I would move into the lower level of Pamela's house, where she was still living with her husband and kids.

Yes, you read that correctly.

I attribute a great deal of my rapid spiritual awakening and self-awareness to living in that house. The home was situated on a large thirteen-acre plot of land in the Virginia countryside. I was surrounded by trees, wildlife and deafening peace and quiet—especially at night.

It took time but I began to look at things differently. A strong sense of discernment became an ally on more and more occasions. It was while living there that I first experienced a profound spiritual connection to nature and the earth. I gained a great understanding of the nature of energy—both positive and negative—while living in that environment. With heightened senses, I recognized that I was an empath and had developed the ability to take onto myself others emotions and pain while also being able to alleviate pain and suffering another might be carrying around. At first, I found that to be a bizarre coincidence—until I began to physically feel the twitches and heat pulsing in my hands as I was asked to alleviate a headache or other physical pain.

Living in that environment was a vital time for developing a growing acceptance of others, as well as myself. It was where I found unconditional love and acceptance. Eventually, it became the first house that I would call *home* since I was eighteen years old. I called that home, *Sanctuary*.

Pamela's husband was still living in the house—which will undoubtedly seem strange to many. For the most part, it was not strange to us, and it wasn't long after I moved in that they divorced. They had followed the path that I had been expected to follow. They had been friends for years prior to getting married, had both graduated from college, were gainfully employed and—as happens far too often—expected to marry, have children and live happily ever after. They loved each other just as my wife and I had loved each other. But it wasn't *the* love that they'd hoped for or expected.

Pam's ex continued to live in the house after their divorce. He did his own thing—dating, living the bachelor lifestyle—while Pam and I did our own thing. Their kids had the benefit of having both parents in the same household while I was the slightly odd uncle. My own children had cut off all communication with me, so I was a surrogate parent to Pam's kids in many ways. Over time, it became clear that one of the reasons that I was guided to be in the home was her children. The family dynamics had me being the 'man in the middle.' Coincidentally, both kids were also spiritually open and in need of direction. In another one of those irony of ironies, I was the one to provide some direction when asked.

We all lived together in that house for eight years. Pam and I were married four years after we'd first met and continued to live there another four years.

There was always one song—another Jimmy Buffett tune—that I couldn't sing or listen to without feeling uneasy. After eight years—the longest I'd lived in any one place since high school—I was able to listen to the song and smile. It wasn't the house itself, it was the acceptance by those living there—especially my butterfly, Pam—that made that house a home.

> *The days drift by*
> *They don't have names*
> *And none of the streets here look the same*
> *And there aren't many reasons I would leave*
> *Yes, I have found me some peace*
> *Yes, I have found me a home.*
> —I Have Found Me a Home (Chorus) by Jimmy Buffett

I lost nearly everything, yet I learned this: Even though it meant leaving behind social norms, I gained that one thing on which life and every spiritual journey must be grounded—unconditional love.

To quote Hawkins again, "The more we give love, the greater our capacity to do so."

Unconditional love isn't elusive. Spirituality isn't elusive. We are all spiritual beings inhabiting a physical vessel—our bodies. The kicker is that until we are shown unconditional love—and recognize it—we can't genuinely love ourselves unconditionally. And, until we can accept ourselves as deserving of that love we are forever searching for that 'one thing' that is situated smack dab in our laps.

Immediately after recognizing what unconditional love feels like, I looked at everything through a new pair of eyes. I was wide awake. My life suddenly had meaning and I had work to do.

That work would have never been possible had I not experienced unconditional love and—more importantly—recognized it. Pamela carried unconditional love along to the winery that day and I gulped it down on a cracker with Brie cheese. It was within me—part of my true self—from that moment.

It was time to go to work. Now, where should I go?

It wouldn't take long for that question to be answered. And, as usual, that answer came in the most unlikely way.

10

PASSION AND PURPOSE

HEARING BON JOVI'S *It's My Life* stands out as the first time I can recall thinking, *Hey, dumbass, ya think that maybe someone is trying to get your attention?* The signs that I was 'under construction' or, 're-construction' began to show up much more often.

I was at a big crossroads in my life now. Not just in terms of what to do for work and a career, but—this was the even harder part—how to know which way to go. What career path should I pursue, now that my old life just didn't seem to fit anymore? And at a much deeper level, who was I? Not at the level of personality, but at the level of core identity?

I had the vaguely dawning sense that I was not supposed to go in some traditional direction as far as my life's work was concerned.

And here I'd thought that being an artist wasn't traditional . . .

In fact, looking back I could see that the signs pointing me in an unusual direction had been there all along—even though, under pressure, I'd let my life and more importantly my mind and spirit be dragged in another direction. The direction of conforming to some sort of outer-world consensus of what life should be and how men should act.

But yeah, the signposts pointing in another direction were already there.

One signpost event had occurred many years in the past, and remained etched so deeply into my mind that I remember every detail of the events of that evening. It was early evening when the phone rang. This was long before mobile phones—you know, the 1980s—and I was home with my girlfriend at the time. I don't recall what she and I were doing, but I imagine that we probably weren't watching television. On the other end of the line, my father's voice softly beckoned, "Jeff, you should come to the hospital. Your grandma doesn't have much time."

My grandmother and I had always been extremely close. Some of my earliest childhood memories are of her and those wonderful Sunday afternoon lunches. Now, I was eighteen years old—within a few weeks of graduating from high school. My life was ahead of me but I knew that hers was slipping away. I had been the apple of her eye since the day I'd been born. She adored my girlfriend—a girl I once thought I'd marry (youthful thinking)—so I asked her to ride with me to the hospital.

I simply said, *"Okay"* in response to my father's words. I knew what was happening. Weeks earlier my grandmother had fallen ill while on a cruise ship. Until that moment, she'd shown no symptoms of the cancer that had consumed most of her brain. She was a strong, proud woman who wouldn't hesitate to show compassion but wouldn't consider burdening anyone with complaints of sickness.

Within minutes I was driving towards Winston-Salem, North Carolina from my home in Lexington—a short thirty to forty-minute trip. My girlfriend, Janet, sat in silence in the passenger seat.

We stayed in the hospital room for a short while. She had

undergone emergency surgery in hopes of removing the tumor and her head was wrapped in white bandages. Yet, she looked at me as I entered and smiled while softly saying, "Hey Shug, it's good to see you. I'm glad you came." The love in her eyes and in her words filled my heart with both joy and sorrow. She had accepted her fate and she was smiling. I was unsure what to say or do. I ached inside.

A short time later, my girlfriend and I left the hospital room and walked in silence from the building to my car. I was visibly shaken, I suppose, because Janet offered to drive back to Lexington. We sat in silence in the car for a moment before she turned to me and asked, "Are you okay?"

Turn on the radio. I'm okay.

Where had those words come from?

I nodded, but the tears welling in my eyes betrayed the truth. I knew I'd never see my grandma again.

Maybe to comfort me, Janet reached out and turned on the radio—and I lost my composure. The message that flowed from the speakers was undeniably directed to me.

The music . . . it had always been music . . . the beauty of sound, the vibration that carried the message.

I recognized the song from the very first notes—*"Every Breath You Take"*—by The Police.

I fell to my left, my head hitting Janet's lap. I knew without a shred of doubt that at that moment, my grandmother had passed away. I also *knew* that my grandma had cued *"Every Breath You Take"* at that moment. The message I received was crystal clear. Yes, I knew that the song was about a subject unrelated to what was happening. But for me the words had an entirely different meaning than what the songwriter intended.

Every step you take, every move you make, every breath you take I'll be watching you . . .

Forever after, when I'd hear that song, I would think of that night, raise my head and smile, knowing that my grandmother was with me—just as if she'd never left.

As years passed, the song—though now a classic Police hit—was played on the radio less and less. The Police had been my favorite band long before that night. I'd seen them perform live long before they were mainstream. When *'Every Breath You Take'* was first released, I thought it was an okay tune but it wasn't my favorite song in their catalogue—a collection of music ranging from the obscure—ever hear of *Brimstone & Treacle*?—to the familiar pop hits most everyone knows by heart. Despite the vast number of songs in that collection, I'd notice that I'd hear *'Every Breath You Take'* at times when I needed comfort—like the day my father died suddenly of a heart attack—or whenever I'd felt alone. My one, true fear had always been a fear of being alone—a feeling I'd struggled to understand for several years during my first marriage. Each time I'd hear the melody, a single verse or the entire song, I somehow knew with certainty that I wasn't alone—my grandmother was close.

Eventually, as more unusual events took place, I would encounter her presence in greater detail and enhanced clarity.

Looking back, I began to realize that so many of those signals were glaring. How I'd missed them at first, I had no idea. Appropriately, it was—and would forever be—music that spoke to me in the most powerful way. It would not be until a few years after I'd met Pam that I became aware of how powerfully music had forever squeezed me like a tube of toothpaste, pushing my spirit—my authentic self—to the top of the tube.

Now that I think of it, one of the things I'd planned was to see the Police in concert on their final reunion tour—with Pam. Coincidence? No such thing.

So, there was the unusual, which I experienced more and more the longer I lived outside the boundaries. Nature as numbers. Days in colors. Messages in music. And a wide-openness in Pam's and my life together. I was starting to see how conforming to the consensus reality had pressed me into a career path that had always fit like a too-tight, plaid leisure suit I wouldn't have chosen for myself.

Since Pam's home was in the country, I spent countless hours outdoors. I walked for miles—what I called 'walking meditations.' I listened to the wind, the rain and the animals. Thunderstorms rolled in and I'd stand in the field, arms reaching to the sky, giddily yelling, "*Bring It! Bring it!*" just as I'd done many months earlier. I became grounded in a way I'd never experienced before.

The energy flowing all around me and coursing through my body was rapidly becoming exponentially stronger.

One night, as Pamela and I lay in bed, she asked if I would put my hand on her forehead. She had a headache that had pestered her for nearly two days. I was lying on the bed to her right. Extending my left arm, I rested my palm on her forehead. There was a throbbing above her right eye that I clearly sensed in my thumb.

I'd laid my hand lightly on her head, mostly to offer comfort. To my surprise, though, the throbbing began to move away from my hand. It was like a game of hide and seek. I followed the throbbing from one eye to the other, to each temple and up to the hairline.

My hand was extremely warm and tingling. I became aware that it was very warm in the room and that I was sweating.

It's rather difficult to describe what happened next. It was as if the pain she'd been experiencing *jumped* from her head into my hand and flowed slowly up my left arm. Without giving it a second thought I raised my left index finger and pointed towards the window. The flowing sensation reversed, causing my hand to tingle even more intensely as I held an intention in my mind that the pain was being released back to the earth.

It sounds strange—even unbelievable—but it happened. My thought—my only intention—the entire time was to bring relief to Pamela.

It was then that everything suddenly made sense to me that. As is theorized in quantum physics—everything is fluid and a form of energy. Thoughts, emotions, intentions, salad tongs, human beings, water—pain—are all energy taking various forms. Energy is everlasting and can't be destroyed or even banished, but negative energies, such as pain, can be renewed—cleansed the way mud can be cleansed from a stream by a current of pure-flowing fresh water.

Pam was a bit taken aback but not surprised. If anything, she was impressed. She told me that I had taken her headache away and that she had felt it moving as my hand 'chased' it from one place to another. For me, it was another one of those *'huh, that's different'* moments.

It was only a matter of a few days before I'd enroll in a Reiki course at Pam's urging. I'd never heard of Reiki and had no idea what to expect when I arrived for my first class. I worked as a bartender at the time, and hadn't returned home until after 3:00AM the night before the 9:00AM class on a Saturday morning. I was tired, but listened as the Reiki Master instructor explained Reiki, its origins and uses. A part of me was skeptical, especially when the subject turned to auras. I'd never been able to see auras around people despite having followed the directions I'd read in books and online. Nonetheless, one of the exercises required each class participant to stand before a white wall while the others attempted to see the aura of the standee.

Seven class members had stood against the wall. As expected, I didn't see colors. I only noticed a few cases of 'bed head' and awkward smiles.

You doubted . . . but hey, that's human nature.

Having waited until the end of the exercise it was now my turn to stand against the wall. The seven other class members looked at me with a focused gaze. A few did a head tilt with one eye squinted as if examining a piece of art hanging on the wall. Others nodded as if they'd noticed something—probably my own case of 'bed head.' Suddenly, two ladies simultaneously blurted out, "I see every color. He has a rainbow surrounding his head and flowing down his shoulders."

The instructor agreed. She'd apparently seen the same thing but didn't want to influence the others.

I was a bit dumbstruck. It would be one thing if it had been one person but two people had seen a plethora of colors, three if counting the Reiki Master instructor.

Coincidence? Hmmmm . . . . No such thing.

The Reiki 1 class lasted an entire day—9:00AM until 6:00PM. During the class I was initiated to the energy through a process called attunement. Afterwards, we were given the opportunity to practice the hand positions and focusing of intention.

Still, some of what I was learning made sense, other aspects seemed, well, goofy. It wasn't until I was instructed to practice giving Reiki that I recognized similarities with my experience with Pam and her elusive headache. The instructor's husband—schooled in Reiki at the Advanced level but not yet a Reiki Master—was my guinea pig. Yeah, it was an intimidating moment. This guy was one level away from Reiki Master, so I was the *'grasshoppah'* and he was the Sensei.

He laid on the table. After going through the steps necessary to prepare myself to be used as a vessel for the betterment of this man, I placed my right hand on my stomach just below the ribcage and used my left hand to 'scan' his body. With my hand six inches above his body, I began at the crown of his head, moving my hand down his body to the soles of his feet and back up the other side of his body, returning to the crown of his head. What struck me as odd while doing this was that as I moved my hand over certain places my hand would feel a coolness, excessive warmth or extreme tingling. When I found these spots, I would stop and lightly place my hand on the area. The most attention was given to his left knee. Three times I returned to that knee until the tingling subsided. I noticed that I was extremely hot and sweat dripped from my brow.

That's odd . . . I was only walking around a table, not doing jumping jacks.

When class was over and everyone was heading for the exit the gentleman approached me.

"Hey," he said, "my left knee has been aching from arthritis for weeks. I've been considering visiting an orthopedist but it feels good now. You know what you're doing. Thank you."

From that moment, I knew that my life was going to become even more interesting. Nearly four years later I completed my Reiki Master certification. I had taken the Reiki 1, 2, Advanced Reiki, and the Master courses, as well as a course in Mindfulness Meditation which Pam and I both completed.

One truth came very clearly to me during that time.

The intention to provide relief and betterment must come from deep inside and it must be rooted in love—a deeper, *spiritual* love and concern. Otherwise, it's nothing more than going through the motions—not unlike a Sunday morning ritual. When the intention is clear and rooted in a genuine love, there is an ability to provide betterment and healing, not only to people but to the earth and every living creature. That revelation was a crucial element to grasp, and opened the way for the path I was on to continue full-speed.

During these studies, I began to assist others with healing, both in person and at a distance. That was a surprise—but then, as quantum physics tells us, we are all interconnected by a web of energy over which intention can move at the speed of light.

One night I was chatting with a friend online. She lived in Maine and had terrible pains in her arms and shoulders. She asked if I could help. Amazingly, after ten short minutes, she typed that her pain was gone.

Oh yes, another crucial element—the one receiving Reiki must be open to receiving and give permission. Having trust and belief also require an expenditure of energy. Not being open to receiving closes the door and nothing positive can result, no matter how pure the intention to help may be—another lesson learned early in my desire to help others.

Being a Reiki Master wasn't my profession, however. I was still stumbling along, not on the path of inner reality and truth, but on my outer path. I now held a sales position with a wine distributor. It was seemingly the ideal position for me and I was quite successful. Still, I didn't get a sense of fulfillment despite being able to sample wine five days a week beginning as early as 9:00AM.

And as for energy and healing work—well, I was just dabbling at it part-time.

Then, one evening I received a phone call from my sister. My father had passed away from an unexpected heart attack. That event caused me to seriously re-evaluate what I was doing to add value, not only to my own life but to the lives of others. To make a long story a bit shorter, I left that industry and became a bar manager—a position I loved simply because I met so many people. And like one might see on television, I had several opportunities to help others, usually through listening and conversing. I was once referred to as the 'Bill Engvall of bartenders' for my humorous takes on life and love. The money was very good and allowed Pam and I to travel to Cancun, Mexico where we spent time at the ancient Mayan ruins at Chichen Itza.

We hadn't planned to visit the ancient site when we traveled to Mexico but while at Chichen Itza, I felt an unbelievable surge of energy and a belonging to the land. I didn't understand what I was feeling at the time but it had an undeniable pull on me and Pam as well. My awareness was flourishing and it was as if I was being guided to places where I could expand my understanding of the connection we all share.

The bar manager position called for long hours and a great deal of manual labor—not to mention twelve-plus hours of being on my feet. Despite the money, I resigned within two years strictly for health reasons. For months, I didn't work. I had plenty to do but those things didn't provide income.

Feeling as if I wasn't contributing as I should, I submitted a resume in response to an ad posted on Craigslist. I was promptly contacted by the company's regional manager and within days I was on a plane bound for Los Angeles and an interview to sell *gulp* LED lighting. The promise of a six to seven figure income was heavily touted throughout the interview process. It would be the last 'professional' career position I'd ever take. However, it was also the position that threw open the drapes and fully illuminated the path to another phase of my spiritual journey. In a bizarre twist of fate interwoven with extreme irony, I discovered what may be the most important aspect of the process of gaining an awareness of self and spirit.

It is amazing what one can hear while in total silence.

My new professional sales position turned out to be a whopper of a pyramid scheme. The only good thing I can say about that job is that it required me to make a move to Florida. I left Virginia on a cold February day and drove to Cocoa, Florida. At the time, I had every intention of becoming successful in the business world again. I had an image in my mind of being on the phone with Pam and telling her to turn in her resignation at work, because I'd secured the financial freedom that ensured a comfortable retirement.

Tell them about the beauty of irony.

Okay. So, I had long ago broken free from the shackles of organized religion. Now, as I embarked on another leg of my spiritual journey, I would be living with extended family—all of whom were devout Jehovah's Witnesses.

The decision to take up residence with Tim, Pamela's cousin, was deliberate. At some time in the past, Tim had also been diagnosed as suffering from Bipolar Disorder. He and his wife had recently separated and he was alone most of the time. Work was sporadic. His teenage son, also a Jehovah's Witness, lived with his mother and would live with Tim a few days each week. At that time, I was still taking medications and had, for lack of a better term, become a 'go-to' source as a bipolar success story. Our shared 'illness' made us brothers-in-arms, I suppose.

I didn't know what to expect when I first arrived at Tim's home. I felt a bit anxious, no doubt. I was 800 miles from Pam, beginning a new career in an unfamiliar place and under tremendous pressure to succeed. On top of that, I had girded my loins in preparation for the possible spiritual sparring session with people who were highly active in a religious sect that I considered to be teetering on the edge of cultism.

It is crystal clear that I was meant to learn a lesson or two about myself, where I was headed, and what I needed to get there. Ironically, living amongst of a group of Jehovah's Witnesses was exactly what I needed to find a very important sense of solace by finding my way to the center of my Self. Several circumstances came together beautifully during those few months in Florida that contributed to my ever-burgeoning spiritual awareness.

Tim had a television in his home. Not once was it on while I stayed with him. Like Tim, I would occasionally watch a movie on Netflix. I had an iPod, headphones and a small speaker. Music was a constant companion for me while I was at the house. Otherwise, it was deafeningly quiet.

Despite the drawbacks of the job, it did provide an enormous perk. The ocean was never more than a few minutes away. On weekdays—usually at lunchtime—I'd find a beach access parking spot, kick off my shoes, roll up my pants and find a spot in the sand to sit, watch and listen as the breakers rolled ashore. When the weekend rolled around, the beach was my sanctuary. I didn't realize at the time that I was learning not only the importance of listening to that little voice inside but how to quiet my mind so that I *could* listen.

What I was noticing inside me was . . . *peacefulness*. I became peaceful with myself, just the way I was. Whether I become a "success" again in anyone's eyes was not the important thing.

Are you at peace with yourself?

The voice was loud and clear, and the wave of energy I rode on was strong when I answered.

"Yes. I am now."

In that state of being, I saw that I'd accepted this new career venture for the wrong reasons—ego again—but gained the realization that I didn't want the noise of the world back in my life. Day after day, I'd find myself sitting in the sand watching the breakers lap against the shoreline. The sea breeze replaced the static of the television. Seagulls were seemingly everywhere.

Before long, silence became my friend, music my muse, the ocean my refuge—and solitude the great open space in which my spirit could move unhindered.

As for the family I was living with—quite likely they'd seen the crystals, incense, candles and the small, smiling Buddha statuette on the window sill. And maybe that was the reason I was never targeted for conversion. Each time I would see Tim enter the living room dressed in suit and tie—prepared for either an evening at Kingdom Hall or a few hours of knocking on doors to spread the good news—I expected a sales pitch for my salvation. It wasn't until the last five minutes before I climbed into my car for the long drive back to Virginia that I was approached—not for a conversion or a salvation sales pitch but for a simple invitation to visit a Kingdom Hall during Easter. That was it. I'd girded my loins for nothing.

For a while, I'd look back at that period and kick myself for having been so damned gullible at having taken the bait—hook, line and sinker—by accepting that job. I'd feel sick when I thought of how much money Pam and I had invested in that promise of a golden financial future. Most often, I'd feel shame and the sinking feeling of having failed Pam.

I now look back and see everything that happened—from the discovery of the career opportunity on Craigslist to my living in Florida with a family of Jehovah's Witnesses—as a series of events that prepared me for an enormous spiritual growth spurt.

When I left Florida the static that had clouded my mind for so very long was gone. After my return to Virginia I would cringe when the television was on. Commercials were especially painful—like needles piercing my ear drums and brain. The same holds true to this day. I'd changed. I stopped running from the quiet and began embracing the stillness—a dramatic shift in awareness accompanied that change.

A few observations that emerged from the stillness, silence, and solitude:

Tim always smiled. Even if his life seemed to be unraveling, he smiled. He knew that everything would be okay.

That showed me everyone has the capacity to find inner peace, so important for healing and moving ahead in life.

Though organized religion in and of itself is a behemoth of a control mechanism, not everyone involved in organized religion will remain forever under its spell. Sure, Tim was spellbound. But, he was also spiritually open and searching.

That showed me everyone is spiritual. Everyone has the capacity to grow to a fuller potential.

Most important, during the time of quiet and open space, a powerful and very strange surge of energy had steadily flowed through me.

Upon returning to Virginia, I stopped taking bipolar medications—cold turkey—with no ill effects. I didn't drop dead at

9:00AM as I'd been warned years ago. Neither were there changes to my behavior, which meant I was taking them for no good purpose.

My mind was now clear, and my senses were sharpened. I quickly became a tremendously sensitive empath.

It was within a week or two of my return home, in fact, that I first noticed these new faculties with striking intensity.

I had traveled into town to take care of some business at the county courthouse. As I walked through the courtyard that was situated between two main buildings others approached me, headed in the opposite direction. There were also people behind, following me to the same building. As the ones approached, I had sickening feelings of dread, sadness, anxiety and hopelessness. I wasn't experiencing those emotions myself.

I was taking those emotions from those individuals who surrounded me.

I cringed. I put a hand on my stomach to quell the queasiness that I was feeling. It wasn't until I'd climb back into my car roughly thirty minutes later that I'd catch my breath.

What the hell was that about?

In addition, I was hot. All the time—hot, sweating—even outside during the winter months. That was only the beginning, when it came to connecting energetically with other people.

It became difficult for me to walk through a building without feeling the emotions and pains—even physical pains—of others as we passed whether inside a room or outside on a sidewalk.

Don't even ask about Christmas shopping at the mall....Impossible.

With awareness came abilities that seemed, well, bizarre. My soul's journey and my soul's purpose was coming into focus. As the focus sharpened, so did my connection to something much, much greater than anything I'd ever imagined—the very source of that inner spark that had fought to break through muck—*spirit itself.*

44

WELL, THAT WAS DIFFERENT

WITHOUT DOUBT, this is the stretch of road that is the most challenging to put into words.

How does one begin in describing the indescribable? I've spent countless hours struggling with the question, *how do I put these experiences into words?* This, despite knowing that those experiences—and those associated with the experiences—are real and in some cases, tangible?

I have come to a place that is personally and spiritually sacred. Sacred in that I have graciously been provided profound insight into my soul's purpose—the underlying reason for this rollercoaster ride. Had I not surrendered and learned to listen, those insights would have been overlooked or ignored—just as they had been for so many years. I've somehow beaten the odds and survived. Having endured physical, emotional, and spiritual upheaval during my journey to wholeness has strengthened me in many ways. Yet, if I sit a moment and consider where I might be had I not surrendered, I shudder.

I no longer believe in coincidence. It wasn't by chance that I happened upon the woman who mentioned that she was a shaman. That brief encounter led me to discover shamanism. Discovering shamanism led to the shamanic journey—a practice that has allowed me to discover that sacred place where inner peace, a connection to self, spirit, and my soul's purpose reside.

The shamanic journey.

Every book I'd read or website I'd studied while researching shamanism listed numerous methods of undertaking a shamanic journey. While shamans in most cultures used drums and rattles to enter a trance-like state of awareness, others used natural psychedelics such as peyote or elixirs such as ayahuasca. Physical movement and dance, chanting and instruments such as singing bowls that produced various tones induced the trance-like state necessary for a shamanic journey by the shamans in other cultures. Along with directions on *how* to embark on a shamanic journey, there were rules galore—some making perfect sense, others not so much.

I now had the powerful sense that I had been moved from my old life into a new life—one of spiritual openness and profound connection to all living things and to the planet itself, to bring healing to others.

Alright, I thought, when this realization came, *where do I start?*

The amount of information seemed overwhelming.

"From all that I've read," said Pam, "you should do whatever you'd do when you put your hand on my head when I have a headache."

She had a point.

Lightwork—which is how I refer to Reiki—and shamanism—journeying on behalf of others—both required intense focus, clear intention and a *knowing* of the connectedness we all share.

"I read that in almost every culture, the initiation of a true shaman was to either have been struck by lightning, have died, or nearly died. You meet that requirement."

That was true. I'd met that requirement three times alone during our first six months together. The first time was due to an idiotic overdose of—get this—melatonin. It was soon after I'd first proclaimed my love for Pam to my wife. There was a heated discussion that followed and the next day my wife and kids had left for North Carolina without me to spend time with her family at Thanksgiving. The prescribed meds for Bipolar Disorder played a part in the most memorable experience. I can't recall which medication I was taking—*Klonopin, perhaps?*—but it sure as hell made me feel good. A little too good. I woke up in the hospital on suicide watch with a ring of black charcoal residue around my mouth. No, I hadn't attempted to take myself out of this world, I just pushed the envelope a bit too far. The other time, well, I'll just say Evel Knievel had nothing on my daredevil antics and leave it at that. That's a story for another day.

I was still learning to properly prepare for Lightwork. I'd learned the hard way that lack of preparation could be painful. As I grew in my understanding of connectedness, I'd become extremely sensitive to that connection we all share—an em*path*—over which our energies flow to each other. The thing is, energy flows both ways. I could have the clearest, most focused intention to bring betterment to another, but if I hadn't taken time to properly prepare myself and my space, I'd inevitably succumb to the pain and discomfort—physical or emotional—that I had worked to alleviate.

I will forever remember the pain of kidney stones without having had kidney stones.

Since I wasn't clued in to a common method of preparation

for a shamanic journey, I prepared much like I would if doing Lightwork. Using sacred symbols for protection, opening, healing, connection and strength—many with similarities to ancient cultural symbols within shamanism—I'd "seal" myself by drawing the symbols over the chakras and both hands. With Lightwork, I'd do this while 'cleansing'—purifying the body and surrendering ego—to become an empty vessel for the light of the Divine.

Next, I'd prepare the space, drawing the same sacred symbols on the four walls, ceiling and floor. While cleansing, I'd begin a type of meditation which I'd carry throughout the Lightwork session. In time, I'd take as long as two hours to prepare for Lightwork.

No more kidney stone pain for me, thank you.

Shamans are acutely aware of 'dark energy'—negative, low vibrational energy that causes dis-ease in the body and mind and can spread like a cancer if not addressed. Raising the vibration of body and spirit to resonate with the highest vibrational frequencies was another practice both shamanic journeying and Lightwork had in common. It was also a practice I'd already been using for quite some time through use of crystals—some of nature's most potent conductors of vibrational energy. For Lightwork, I began to use Quartz, Hematite, Lapis Lazuli, Garnet, Citrine and Malachite—just to name a few—to raise and adjust vibrations. I'd use these during a shamanic journey as well, later adding other natural elements such as wood from a tree that had been struck by lightning.

Now came the journeying.

Following the method for shamanic journeying shared by an author of a book about Western-thought shamanism, Sandra Ingerman's *Shamanic Journeying, A Beginner's Guide*, I added a traditional element necessary for my shamanic journey- drumming.

Easy enough—there's an app for that.

With a drumming app on my phone and headphones plugged

in, I was now equipped for an entirely new type of journey.

As the drumming began, I closed my eyes and covered them beneath a bandana. I'd set the timer on the drumming app for one hour—the maximum allowable—as I had no idea how long it might take to 'start the car', so to speak. In seemingly no time at all, the engine cranked and my first shamanic journey was underway.

Learning to quiet my mind during my time in Florida paid off in more ways than one. Thank you, my Jehovah's Witness friend.

In a matter of moments, a swirling kaleidoscope of colors burst forth in my mind's eye. Shapes, images and outlines of tree lines, people I didn't recognize, cityscapes—all in constantly changing hues—would form then quickly morph into something completely different. The colorful bursts would retreat only to be replaced by another, then another. The intensity of the colors grew more brilliant as—at the center of my view—an opening surrounded by brilliant emerald green acted as a window. It was if I was looking through myself—through time itself—at a place I'd seen before. I could still feel the bed under me and the crystals I held in each hand. Yet, an aspect of me wasn't in the room. My consciousness was in two distinct places—my everyday conscious was in a body, while my higher self was standing on the shoreline of a stream. Across the stream stood a massive tree, its base deeply rooted within bright green grass and a broad, multi-colored canopy containing thousands upon thousands of branches, reaching upwards towards a sky illuminated by three moons. Beyond the tree were mountains—the source of the stream—and behind me was a vast field of sunflowers. I knew the place, although it wasn't as I remembered it when I was a young boy. It was the backyard of my childhood home. I was overcome by a sense of acceptance and welcoming.

I was home.

The drumming changed, abruptly sending me soaring back to where I'd started my journey. Sixty minutes had elapsed yet it seemed as if I'd been away much, much longer.

Now, how was I going to be able to describe what I'd experienced in those sixty minutes to Pam?

Jibrail was the name of the very first 'being' that I encountered during the journey. A commanding presence with a seriousness emanating from his essence. Golden light fading outwards into brilliant white—reminiscent of diamonds in sunlight—swirled, flowed and spun around me—my higher self. I later described it as being caught in water spout and able to see every glistening droplet pass by. Though serious and stern, Jibrail's presence was warm and comforting.

I didn't recognize the name though it had a hint of familiarity. Jibrail, I'd later learn, is the Arabic form of the name, Gabriel—as in *the* Gabriel—the Archangel who'd delivered the message to the Virgin Mary that she would have a child.

Gabriel had been known to me only as Gabriel since childhood. Even then, I had a difficult time grasping the idea of heavenly, winged beings. I'd never heard of Jibrail before that shamanic journey. It was during that initial shamanic journey that Jibrail directed me to tell my story so that others "may learn and grow without fear." There was a palpable sense of urgency in the message:

"Humanity is destroying itself. The divinity within is being swallowed by the shell. There must be balance. Without balance, *all* is altered."

Uh, how? What do I tell? I've never written anything.

I clearly understood Jibrail's directive. Yet, the moment

I returned from the journey, my mind was flooded with questions. I didn't verbally ask questions while in Jibrail's presence. Questions were answered without my needing to ask. The message resonated with my soul. Still, my unspoken questioning of his directive warranted a very succinct response.

"The words have been written, the story told. Listen. Discern. Trust. Share. The words will become a beacon—the light that awakens many."

The response made perfect sense to me . . . the next day. When I fully understood the message and its implied urgency, it was like I'd been given a gentle nudge by a parent on the very first day of school. At that moment, I began to mentally write my story.

Jibrail/Gabriel became the essence of discernment and communication in every form—verbal, physical, written, unspoken, gestured, intentions and visual. It was Gabriel who would enhance my growing understanding of those forms of communication, whether I was the one communicating or receiving the messages. Many times, the messages presented themselves in the lyrics of a song, an article I'd be reading, a repeating sequence of numbers or the presence of an animal. Other times, the messages came from people I'd meet during a chance encounter and were so blatantly obvious that to consider them to be mere coincidence was out of the question.

It was Jibrail—as well as Raphael—who accompanied me on a shamanic journey to a past life. I was shown who I had been, when and where I had lived, how I had died and why. That journey left an enormous impression on me afterwards.

I watched as a man in what appeared to be his early twenties was dragged to a river. His legs were limp, because they'd been broken. As he was dragged then thrown into the water he gasped for breath each time his head would rise from the water, unable to stay afloat. Shrieks of pain paled in comparison to the terror that was visible in his eyes as he first glimpsed the alligators leaving the brush along the river's shoreline and entering the water. He had been a scribe for an Egyptian official and had been accused and convicted of secretly defying the religious belief of the time. It was a tortuous death penalty for a trusted and valued member of the Pharaoh's hierarchy.

As I watched the penalty, I simultaneously was seeing the scribe's home and family, his daily task as a scribe for the official as well as and his covert action as a scribe for the populace.

What does this mean? Why is this relevant to my life and the world?

Again, my question wasn't spoken but it was answered nonetheless. I was given the name of the scribe—and the name of the scribe's wife—and told that I was to complete what the scribe had begun. I was the scribe who'd played a role in defying a long-held religious belief system for a long-dead pharaoh.

Take a moment to let that sink in. I certainly did.

The entire journey was not only overwhelming but it seemed a bit outrageous. By this time, returning from a journey and going to the internet to search for names or other bits of information I'd received had become second nature. The expression on my face surely resembled a boy in puberty thumbing through *Playboy* magazine for the very first time, when I not only found the scribe's name but the Pharaoh of the time, the Pharaoh prior who had introduced the idea of a different theology, how that scribe had perished and—get this—the name of the scribe's wife. All this information—documented by historians—was staring back at my dropped-jaw, bug-eyed face.

There are no coincidences. There are no coincidences. There are no coincidences.

The story I'd been directed to share—the trials, tribulations and triumphs—was to be a conclusion to what that scribe had started in that time. Amazingly, many circumstances of that time were strikingly similar to those I'd been seeing played out around the world and in my own hometown.

Other shamanic journeys introduced me to other beings— essences of the Divine—for various reasons. Raphael—I refer to Raphael as my compadre—first presented himself (I use the masculine description due to his always presenting a masculine appearance or essence), in what I came to refer to as my 'sacred landing zone,' that place of peace, beauty and balance I'd first visited and met Jibrail.

I knew that the journey held a strong message whenever I'd notice that the trunk of the majestic tree wasn't wood but two enormous, intertwined pythons or the canopy was changing color or form—often flames—as a symbolic message.

Raphael was and would continue to be the being who'd assist with healing during my Lightwork and with my personal physical, emotional and spiritual betterment. Raphael also presented his essence in nature through wind, clouds and the elements.

As my journeys continued, I encountered other celestial, divine beings. With the one exception being Archangel Michael, none were previously known to me. Each met me in that sacred place or I was taken to them for help or information pertaining to aspects of a journey.

Haniel, Zadkiel, Uriel, Cassiel, Chamuel, Jophiel—just to name a few—met me one or more times. Each one had an essence that emanated from a different color or vibration and delivered a specific message.

After each journey I'd jump to research a name I'd been given. Each time I'd do the research, *bada-bing, bada-boom*, there was the name, often in italics and boldface type, just as I had discovered after my encounters with Jibrail and the scribe.

As if this weren't enough . . . .

It was on January 3rd, the day after I'd arrived in Charlotte, North Carolina, to visit my sister and mother that my life would *again* forever change.

My sister was scheduled for hip surgery that week and I had driven down south to stay with her and—because she lived alone with only three dogs, two of which were blind and another I'd dubbed 'Nutjob' due to his extreme enthusiasm—help her through the early stages of the recovery process.

The night before, I'd downed a glass or four of wine after arriving. Traffic had been brutal, I'd been driving in the dark—something that had become more difficult for some odd reason—and I was tired. Together, they were the ingredients in the recipe for a reason to 'relax' and 'unwind' with some hearty cabernet.

I'd brought with me the objects that I would normally use whenever I'd embark on a shamanic journey—crystals, earth elements, essential oils, and earphones for the drumming app that resided on my cellphone—with the assumption that I might have a need to journey or just to use while meditating.

That 3rd of January was sunny with temperatures in the 60s—pleasant compared to Northern Virginia. Much of the day was spent feverishly lazing on the sofa, catching up with my sister or reading. For Christmas, Pam had gifted me with a collection of DVDs—the entire collection of Dean Martin Roasts—and I'd toted them to Charlotte. That evening, my sister and I watched and laughed as tears of laughter streaked our faces. I briefly had a moment of pride as I realized that I'd not had any wine that day or night.

Huh.

At some point late in the evening, I had a 'nagging'—that's the best way I can describe the sudden interruption of laughter—a call to journey. I didn't have a reason, wasn't asked by anyone and I hadn't planned to journey for any specific reason so I was a bit confused.

Not long after the 'nagging,' I retreated to the confines of the guestroom, unsure what to do. What would be my intention?

I can't journey without an intention, can I?

I gathered my toiletries and camouflage designer sleepwear and headed to the guest bathroom across the hall. I'd become accustomed to showering in the evening and always before and after journeys. That night, I was covered with cleanliness whether I journeyed or not.

There was something about the nagging feeling that I was to journey that night that I hadn't experienced prior to my other travels. So, with no definite intention other than to journey to my 'landing zone,' I lit a tea light candle, placed it in the diffuser I'd filled with purified water, added Frankincense, Myrrh and Clary Sage essential oils and hoisted the anchor. As I was lying on the bed, my earbuds filled my ears with the entrancing sounds of double drums and rattles. I began to sink into an ocean of energy . . . .

All That is, The Divine, God, Source. The Light.

The Light was a beacon I followed.

When I arrived in my sacred space—my 'landing zone'—the surroundings were slightly different. The water was a brilliant aqua color, the sunflowers reaching to the sky. A figure approached from the other side of the stream with a casual stride. Oddly, the figure appeared as a shadow, as if backlit but shining with a brilliance so great it dazzled my eyes.

Standing on the opposite side of the stream stood a figure—an essence that emanated pure love, warmth and acceptance. The presence was welcoming and beckoned me to come closer. The stream had widened and was deeper, the streambed below shone with glints of golden light. I moved forward and was immediately submerged in the deep, aqua stream. I sank deeper, aware of what was happening. It was a cleansing—much like the biblical baptisms that John the Baptist performed in the River Jordan or, the cleansing I'd perform prior to Lightwork. I continued to sink without care when an arm plunged into the water, grasped me and pulled me upwards and free from the stream. I wasn't wet, I wasn't afraid and I certainly wasn't expecting to encounter Raphael, the one who'd pulled me from the stream.

The cleansing was complete, but why was it necessary?

It hadn't been Raphael that I'd first seen on the other side of the stream. The essence of purity that had walked to the stream was the essence of a being that I'd abandoned during my upheaval. As quickly as a hummingbird flaps its wings, the essence became a figure. The questions *Who are you?* and *What's happening here?* rose simultaneously with the answer.

"My name is Yeshua. Come with me."

Like with the others, I'd not heard of the name Yeshua. However, I had heard the name Jesus used many thousands of times.

Yeshua—Jesus—I'd later learn is known as an ascended master—an essence who'd once inhabited a human body.

Standing in front of me was the figure of a man—slightly taller than my physical self with a light brown complexion and dark shoulder length hair. His demeanor was gentle and in his eyes and smile was the epitome of acceptance. His appearance didn't remotely resemble the pictures of a fair skinned Jesus—looking upward to the left, his right—that adorned the wall of the fellowship hall at every church I'd ever attended.

A flood of questions flowed through my consciousness as Yeshua—the one I'd forever known only as Jesus Christ, the Messiah, Son of God, Son of Man, King of Kings, etc.—whisked me upwards. It was if I was traveling upward at light speed, bursting through thin skins of bubbles along the way.

One ... two ... three ... four ... five .... We've stopped.

What I was to witness required days to process afterwards. However, the message I received in response to my own questions I'd held was concise and answered in a direct manner requiring minimal effort. It was the only 'worded' message I received during this journey.

"I didn't live to establish a religion. Religion is a human creation. Religion easily envelops and divides the light from the light's Source. I was not understood by most, only ones who *listened*. I walked as a messenger. You are now as I was then—human, yet aware of being a vessel for the light of the Divine. Many carried the message before me—many carried the message even as I walked. The light cannot be quelled but it can be dimmed. Look.. ... "

Words weren't exchanged but there was the *knowing* that I'd become accustomed to feeling. I watched as images of spiraling galaxies, solar systems, universes, and multiple overlapping universes—all originating from a single point—spiraled forward into nothingness only to be reborn from the center point. I was seeing this from a vast distance and watching the as if I was wearing 3D glasses. What I was looking at in whole was circular. *The Flower of Life. A spherical, multi-dimensional Flower of Life.*

Sacred Geometry. Numbers. Sunflowers . . . Pam. It all made sense. I was being given knowledge of the structure and workings of things unseen.

I gained an understanding that not only is our tiny slice of the world miniscule in the grand scope of everything, it is beyond miniscule. In cosmic terms, the universe that we consider to be infinite is the size of something an atom would eat as finger food. What I was seeing was giving me an understanding of something as profoundly perplexing as gravity—how it works and is affected by more than the moon and a magnetic field. The overlapping nature of one universe affects the other. Deeper still, the spiraling within each—spiraling that can accelerate or decelerate—is affected by the nature of what is occurring within any single universe.

What difference can a dim light in a few million—even a few billion—human vessels make?

It took me a few days to grasp the depth of the message. I was best able to describe it using imagery.

The light is dimming and throwing our lives and planet out of balance. Like spinning plates on sticks, if one plate begins to wobble, the others wobble. We are on a wobbly plate. If we're on a wobbly plate, anything or anyone that may exist within those other spirals is also on a wobbly plate.

I would often call upon Yeshua for assistance. Those needs for assistance were most times requests for increased patience, tolerance and *knowing*. Yeshua could easily relate to the temptations, trials and pitfalls of life as a human carrying the light of the Divine. In the same way, he taught how to recognize the beauty of everyday life. "There is beauty and light within every situation, every person every moment. Look past what the eyes see."

Look, listen and discern. Oh, and laugh. Humor is the light in disguise. Smiles and laughter are powerful healers.

The evening of January 2nd—the night prior to my encounter with Yeshua—was the last night I'd taste alcohol. Wild Turkey strutted out, cold turkey slipped in. As a result, I left 'careers' selling wine and acting as a bar manager—I'd very much enjoyed and excelled at each—because I'd been directed to not imbibe. I couldn't say, "Uh, I don't think so," to Jesus.

Immediately, drinking no longer appealed to me.

My awareness and spiritual understanding blossomed as the days, weeks and months passed. Shamanic journeys had also introduced me to nature's little helpers—spirit animals—prior to the encounter with Yeshua. Badger was the first I'd bumped into. The Snake, Spider, Frog and even Chipmunk brought messages both in journeys as well as daily waking life. There were others, each presenting a message relating to a given situation, problem or simply for support and encouragement. I began noticing even the smallest insect with a different perspective.

A few months passed. The bone-chilling winter winds that had constantly rattled the windows and piles of shoveled snow from record winter storms began to slow and wither away. Spring was sneaking in through the cracks in the gray clouds. The daylight was getting longer and warmer, the nights shorter and, well, warmer.

Nudge

That little nagging feeling returned one of those days as the trees were shaking off the brown hues and the green returned. I didn't question what I'd felt. The call to undertake an impromptu journey was a bit different—more of a nudging than a nagging—but the *knowing* was there.

Preparation, check. Drumming, check. Quartz, Citrine, Lapis and Malachite, check. Ok, let's do this.

Seated with his back to me was a figure I immediately recognized. "'Bout time . . . what took so long?" Raphael was a jokester at times and all business at times. Most times, he was a bit of both. This was one of those times. During shamanic journeys, I'd encounter Raphael in the form of colors, vibrations, the traditional winged angel but with the tips of each wing a brilliant green, or a simple *knowing* of his presence. Most journeys, his presence was in human form—one familiar to me.

The sky was a brilliant blue, the setting almost blindingly bright although there was no sun. Wearing cargo shorts, a white, sleeveless t-shirt with an arrow that pointed in my direction no matter where I moved and the words, "I'm With It," a barefoot Raphael lifted a finger and placed it in the sand.

"C'mon over. Have a seat." His tone was serious despite his appearance. "Look *there*." The index finger on his left hand pointed to a large pool of water surrounded by a rocky shore. There was a vast expanse of ocean beyond the pool of water.

That's strange. A pond on a beach.

As I looked to the pond of water, I felt a slight breeze. The breeze skimmed across the water, blowing from right to left causing small ripples to form on the pond. The ocean beyond the pond remained serene.

"See how the water moves? The breeze is blowing from only one direction, but the water moves differently. Small ripples—barely visible—move upwards, larger ripples move sideways. Do you see what happens?"

I gazed ahead at the water. The breeze remained steady. The smaller ripples moved slowly upwards as the larger ripples moved from right to left and slightly downward. I didn't immediately make the connection but I didn't need to say so.

Raphael motioned towards a single crest, the largest ripple on the pond. "Watch that one."

The crest, moving more quickly than the smaller ripples, overcame and absorbed the small hills of water. The small ripples were gone and were now moving along at the same pace and direction of the larger crested ripple. The small waves of water were just ... gone. I continued to watch the large crest become larger as it moved across the surface, absorbing the smaller ripples in its path. As it grew larger in size, it increased in speed until it met the rocky shore.

"That wave was a small ripple when the breeze began. Underneath the surface the water is what it is—water. On the surface, the water is the same but the breeze changed its nature."

That makes sense.

"Many small ripples have become a single, cresting wave. No matter the size, each will eventually meet the shoreline. Yet, as the large crests overtake the small ones, the small ripples remain as small parts of something more powerful. The small ripples meet the same fate as the crest that consumed them when they crash into the rocks as a large, fast-moving crest. The ones not overtaken will eventually meet the shore gently or disappear on the water's surface."

With that, the sky darkened and the gentle breeze became a gusty wind.

A single *plop*-sound came from the pond. Behind the pond, a brightness was cast over the serene ocean. Another *plop*, this one making a sound signaling a larger object hitting the pond surface was followed by an increasing number of stones hitting the water.

"Hailstones. Look closely.—What happens to the water as they meet the surface?"

I watched as the hailstones met the water. Some large, some small but all impacting the ripples and causing them to break apart, sending the separated ripples outward in every direction. No large crests were spared. Remarkably, the smaller ripples that had been released from the larger crests just moments earlier flowed into each other from every direction yet none formed large, consuming waves.

"Under the surface, the hailstones melt, becoming part of the pond. They're water, no different than the water they just beat to shreds on the surface."

Beat to shreds?

"It appears that the hailstones create chaos, doesn't it?"

At that moment, it was clear where Raphael was going. The hail hadn't created chaos. It had only appeared to be chaotic and violent on the surface, with a darkened sky as a backdrop. What each hailstone had done as it slammed into the water's surface was just the opposite. The hailstones had liberated the smaller ripples, preventing a metaphorical death by conformity on a rocky shore and allowing them to move in every direction. They couldn't form another large crest as they met others because each was also moving in another direction. The ripples had been freed.

I'm starting to get it. This is making sense.

"You, my friend, are a hailstone—a teacher, a leader, a healer. There are many others. Some are aware, some aren't—yet. Some you'll find, others will find you. Balance must be restored. Remember, under the surface, water is water."

I parted with an understanding of humanity demonstrated by ripples on a pond and a sense of urgency with the knowing that a teacher, healer and leader can be all three without uttering a word, performing brain surgery or becoming president.

It's amazing how many eyes we have if we'll just open one of them and listen, eh?

That spring, I was also given the message, "There will soon come a time of upheaval followed by a short rest before another time of upheaval."

Thank you, Gabriel.

The upheaval did come later that summer, but it was a walk in the park compared to my personal upheaval early in my soul's journey.

42

COMMUNION AND CONFIRMATION

THE TIME HAD COME for each of us living in the house—the only place I'd called 'home' since childhood—to move on and go our separate ways. A large, white realtor's sign was firmly planted at the end of the long gravel drive. I didn't know how long it would be but I knew without doubt that Pam and I would soon be leaving the house and land that I'd dubbed *Sanctuary*. The house was shown numerous times beginning the first day after being advertised. *For Sale—Beautiful, custom-built home on large, secluded lot. Perfect for a large family! Must see!*

My shamanic journeys placed me in the presence of animals more often, each providing direction, protection, assurance and an enhanced connection with nature that had been growing stronger and more intense with each passing day.

Sanctuary went on the market near the beginning of the summer season. In addition to the routine, "keep the house clean, there might be a showing," requirements, I spent a great amount of time outside.

During the heat of summer, I would load hand tools—bowsaw,

axe, clippers, shovel, machete, etc.—into the rear of the truck and drive to the end of the driveway. There I'd park, and take a deep breath before climbing from the truck. Despite being covered head to toe with two layers of clothing, I'd spray myself with bug repellent (Lyme Disease was an ever-present threat), and give a little 'nod to the gods' before I began clearing brush and poison ivy from the heavily wooded land to that ran adjacent to the driveway. I'd catch myself at times talking to the trees as I trimmed away dead limbs, clinging vines of poison ivy and weeds.

There ya go, you're free to grow now. I'd say with a smile.

Or I'd lay my hand on a tree and simply whisper, *Thank you.* I found solace and gratitude in what most would consider an arduous, labor intensive chore and I'd often work until darkness forced me to call it a day—my clothes soaking wet, my hands sore and my soul mended.

I also found peace in mowing the thirteen acres that encompassed the house. Mowing the yard, clearing brush and digging up and hauling large, milky quartz stones to surround the unfinished water hole in the front of the house were activities I'd come to look forward to carrying out.

Near summer's end, an offer to purchase the home was submitted. After some back and forth negotiations and a lot of give and take, Pam and her ex accepted the offer. Just like that, the place I considered Sanctuary—my home for eight years—would soon be occupied by others. What didn't go unnoticed was that the ones who'd purchased the house had something in common with many who'd toured the home. They were a married couple with an elderly parent and an older special needs child. The senior mother was to be in hospice care—which began the day after closing—and the child needed outdoor space.

It was a bittersweet time. So much of my journey had taken

place while living in that home. My soul had been flayed and healed while there. Yet, I'd been given notice some months earlier, "The people do not choose the land, the land chooses the people." The land had chosen those people—that family—for many of the same reasons it had first chosen Pam, and later, me.

"What better place for the mother to transition over to the Light?" I said to Pam. "What better place for someone with special needs to find healing? It's time for us to take what we've learned from our time here and share it with others. These people need this place for reasons we know and reasons we can't see."

The day arrived when I knew that I'd been accepted and had established a tangible and spiritual connection with nature. It was one of those *Lifetime Channel* moments that would cause one to choke up while watching. The moment lasted a minute or two and occurred as I mowed the lawn for the last time before we were to move.

I still marvel at that moment . . . especially how it was the picture-perfect conclusion to an event that occurred a couple of months earlier. Now, that was a more Sci-fi Channel than Lifetime Channel moment.

It was a warm and slightly overcast late summer morning. I'd fueled and fired up the mower, donned the headphones and headed out to give the lawn its weekly crew cut. Most times, I'd begin with the lawn on the densely wooded side of the house—the right side if looking at the house from the road. Never one to run from adventure, that day I mixed it up and began with the left side of the lawn—the side with the lightly wooded area I'd spent hours clearing brush.

The roar of the large mower was muffled and replaced with

the music flowing through the headphones. The sun began to break through the overcast sky causing the thermostat of the late summer morning to quickly rise. The wooded area was situated in the center of a small slice of the property, forming an isosceles triangle of sorts. As I finished the longest side of the triangle, I whipped the mower around the corner and followed the tree line on the back side of wooded area.

Looking ahead, I noticed something in my path. *A limb? Tree stump? I guess I'll find out.* I slowed and navigated the mower to the left of the object as I neared. *It's a deer . . . a baby deer.* I stopped the mower with no more than two feet between the mower and the animal. *Huh . . . that's one brave little fawn.* The mower's engine continued to roar while I looked down on the tiny animal. *Deer usually bed down in tall grass or wooded areas, not like this—not out in the open.* I watched closely for a twitch or the rise and fall of the deer's side as she breathed.

Nothing.

I'd heard from Pam that deer are masters of the 'playing possum' game when cornered much like humans are when cornered by a bear. *Play dead and the threat goes away—that's the theory.* This was different somehow. I cut the engine to the mower, removed my earphones and glasses and climbed from the driver's seat. My gaze didn't leave the fawn as I slowly removed my gloves and inched close to her tiny body. *Get up! C'mon, I'm not gonna hurt ya,* I screamed on the inside. *Nothing. Either she's gone or she's a tiny 'possum' master.*

Her eyes remained closed and her body remained still. And as I knelt beside her body, my right hand instinctively reached out to her lifeless form, coming to rest on her side.

My scalp was tingling . . . there was a high-pitched ringing in my left ear.

There was no rise and fall that would indicate breathing, no thump that would signal a heartbeat and the body was cool to the touch. *She must've been lost, unable to find the others early this morning.* I reached out with my left arm, placing my left hand on her body just underneath my right.

Well, this is different. No . . . no, it isn't. Lightwork is Lightwork. Water is water.

Looking upwards, I closed my eyes and began to silently call on my compadre—Raphael—and the elements around us to bring peace to the tiny creature. As my intention became more focused, my hands grew warmer. My hands didn't move from where I'd placed them. *Warmer . . . warmer . . .*

Thump.

I felt one single movement under the middle finger of my right hand. That was all I felt—one thump—and suddenly she scrambled to her feet.

I stared in disbelief as she stood on unstable legs, turned her head, and looked back at me. Our eyes locked for a split second and in that moment the look in her eyes conveyed a mutual respect—a connection. *Water is water.* It was a look that I'd not forget. The fawn turned her head and slowly began a short, wobbling walk to the recently brush-cleared triangle.

I patted myself down, searching for my phone.

Gotta call Pam. Damn, where is my phone? There it is . . . connected to the other end of my headphones.

With one eye watching the fawn as she rested under a large tree I'd just the day before cleared of thorns and poison ivy and the other on the keypad of my phone, I dialed Pam. I hurriedly tried to tell her what I'd seen—and done.

"I'll be down there in a minute. I'm bringing water." That was her response. No questioning, no incredulous looks as I again described the events after she arrived with the water.

We placed a bowl of water a few feet from the fawn and waited for her to drink. She didn't drink the water but roughly ten minutes passed before she again climbed to her feet, exited the triangle and began walking towards the heavily wooded lot on the other side of the driveway. She walked slowly at first, then faster as she neared the trees. Then, she disappeared into the thickets and darkness of the woods.

Did all of that just happen? Yeah, it happened. That. Just. Happened.

I stood for a few moments more—looking towards the place where the fawn had disappeared—before climbing aboard the mower. I completed the yardwork several hours later. What had started off as a day of appreciating the nature surrounding me ended as a day of solid connection to that nature—and validation that under the surface, water is water.

The roar of the mower's engine was muffled one last time by the music flowing through my earphones. I didn't rush to finish the mowing of the lawn knowing that I'd not be doing it again. We were to move in a few days. My thoughts moved back and forth as I bounced around on the mower. Appreciation, excitement, bittersweet sorrow—all rolled into one big ball of thought and emotion. I'd not spoken to anyone of what had occurred a couple of months earlier.

The days were becoming shorter. My last lap on the mower was nearing as the day had started to fade away. The brightness of the colors of the land were beginning to dim, changing the landscape's colors by adding a splash of yellow and orange. *Two, maybe three more laps—then, that's it.*

I began another lap, heading down the length of the front

lawn towards the road.

Halfway to the road I caught a glimpse of movement to my right. I turned my head without slowing, to look for what had caught my attention. Two deer entered my view, crossing the driveway and stopping in the grass ahead of me.

One buck, one doe, neither yet full grown. Couldn't be . . . nah. Could it?

The buck stopped slightly ahead of the doe, a black stripe running down his back. The doe's coat was light brown with a smattering of white spots. I stopped the mower thirty or so yards from them, engine still roaring. The buck turned to look my way then, with a single leap, jumped the wooden fence that turned into the driveway and disappeared into the woods—the same densely wooded land that the fawn had disappeared into only two months earlier.

The doe didn't follow. I cut the engine. Some thirty or so yards separated us. There it was—that *knowing*. The doe stood firm. With a smile, I softly uttered the words, *"Hello, again."* It was a moment of connectedness in its purest form. The doe's message wasn't lost on me.

It's time to go. You're ready.

Ready for what, I didn't know.

The doe broke our connected gaze, turned her head, and softly walked into the woods, just as she'd done that day two months earlier.

Take care of them, the ones who take our place. My words were barely audible.

I spoke to the land in a whisper, a slight lump in my throat. *Thank you—thank you. I won't forget.*

Later, I related to Pam what had happened. She understood—it was time to let go and step out into a new adventure—a journey to an unknown destination.

The land chooses the people. The land heals. The land provides nourishment for the soul.

Be still, listen and you just might hear your soul whispering, "Pssst, hey you. Yeah, you. I have connections to anything and everything. It's yours, free of charge. All you need to do is listen. Or, we can do this the hard way."

When you get the offer, take the deal. Trust me, you will be glad you did.

EPILOGUE

BEFORE I WAS GUIDED to share my story, I had created an online blog. It was a place of refuge—an outlet—where I could rant, question, and write without judgement during the most tumultuous stretch of road on my journey. I'd dubbed the blog, *Yelps from the Closet*. Many times, I'd begin in the early evening and not stop until rays of the morning light illuminated the room. The blog was a place to vent frustrations, proclaim victories, and lament losses.

I also two-finger typed several satirical items, one of which I described as a chapter of the Bible that had been omitted—the *Book of Leon*—the *faux* biblical account of a pimp in Harlem in the modern day, written in 'jive' vernacular. The blog mixed outrageous and flat out goofy writings with accounts of the trials, tribulations and triumphs of my life. Despite the subject matter, humor was the common thread woven through everything I'd written.

I was surprised when I one day received a comment in response to something I'd written. I'd not been aware that my writings were being read by others. More surprisingly, comments began trickling in from others who related to my travails or simply appreciated the humor I'd infused into otherwise traumatic issues. The humor I'd injected into those rants and ramblings had shone a light on difficulties which seemed, also to my surprise, to resonate with others.

Huh, that's kind of cool, I thought.

Later, I'd find that my blog—my refuge and outlet—was being read by others worldwide. Individuals in China, Russia, England, France, Turkey, India and many other countries were following my writings.

I wasn't expecting this.

The blog led to my being a regular 'personality' on an L.A. Talk Radio program. I was dubbed "The Unholy Reverend", and basically used my voice to elaborate on topics very much like those I'd tackled in my blog—religion, familial frustrations, uncertainty—infusing my comments with copious amounts of humor.

In time, my travels led me to roads with fewer speed bumps. The roads weren't without a pothole here and there but they weren't pock marked with craters. The sleepless nights spent writing dwindled as I began to find peace and a sense of self-acceptance.

Flash forward a few years. Same man, same humor, different person.

Writing about the path I've taken has been by far the most difficult task I've ever undertaken.

I had been guided to share my story with the world. Along the way, I'd been directed to no longer imbibe in my trusty friend cabernet sauvignon or any other alcohol—a directive that I found no difficulty in following. I now know that—had I not followed that directive—I'd not have been able to follow Jibrail's guidance and this memoir would have never materialized.

While pecking away at the keyboard or scribbling on paper the events within this memoir, I didn't stop to think that I might also be one of the ones who could benefit from my story. As I delved into an event, experience or period during that time, I often found that I was continuing to be enlightened. Penning this memoir has been a journey in its own right.

Just when I thought I had it all figured out . . . nope. There's always more to learn.

I'd initially started writing this book with my intention firmly set—*Listen for the words, discern the origin of those words, share my story.* Oddly enough, the final chapter—though difficult to put into words—held the ultimate message I was to convey.

The message is simple, but then nothing is 'simple,' right?

Humanity—a collective word for an entire species. *Underneath the surface, it's all water.* Each of us may originate from a different land, have different color skin, differ in gender, age and size. Any number of other outer characteristics distinguish one from another. In our minds, we may differ in beliefs or opinion on any and every topic. We are each on a journey and though the rest areas and scenic overlooks differ, we all arrive at the same destination.

I hope like hell that most people don't fight along the way as I did.

We're all made of the same stuff—skin, guts and bones. Yet, the fiber of our being is identical. The light inside—the whisper we all hear at some time—comes from the same source and beckons us to listen. *Listen*—not hear and dismiss—to that inner voice, the authentic self—the soul.

Don't become a ripple that succumbs to the cresting wave. *I'd rather die while I'm living than live while I'm dead*—those words resonated with me. What words resonate with you?

It's my life?

Fake It?

Something completely different, perhaps?—a sudden sense of being moved by a soft breeze?

How about a message the strikes you from the middle of a loud infomercial?

Messages come at us from every direction every day and many times they come in the unlikeliest way at the unlikeliest time.

When I began this journey, those words in a Jimmy Buffet song grabbed me by the shoulders and shook me out of a trance.

The lyrics to *Growing Older but Not Up* still speak to me, though now they carry other messages.

Something about broken bones and memory loss, I think.

And though my journey is ongoing, it's only fitting that I end this book with another song.

There are no coincidences—not when you're awake and listening.

Moments after I'd completed the final chapter I arose from my chair, took a deep breath and decided to shower. I'd months earlier created a playlist of music and titled it, *Soundtrack of My Life*. The playlist consisted of more than five hundred songs. Every genre—classical to heavy metal and more—was included. I've always appreciated every form of music. I haven't been a fan of all of them, but I've appreciated them. What speaks to one may not speak to another.

As I waited for the shower water to warm I powered on my speaker and chose my *Soundtrack* playlist and pressed the 'shuffle' option. Just as the shower door closed behind me, the opening notes of a song—another Jimmy Buffett tune which rarely played—softly pierced the sound of running water. In a split second, it was if I'd been given the 'thumbs up' in recognition of my having followed the guidance and directives I'd been given so many months earlier.

The song, *Pacing the Cage*, was one I'd first heard years earlier in the very place in time I'd found myself gazing from the bedroom window. I'd always forwarded the song. It was a ballad—beautiful yet slow—and I was at a *'Margaritaville'* age at the time.

Yet, on that day as the shower door closed and the soothing water cleansed my mind and body, *I listened*. I was overcome with emotion, laughing and sobbing simultaneously. I lifted my head, looked upward, smiled and softly whispered, "*Thank you.*"

Pacing the Cage

Sunset is an angel weeping
Holding out a bloody sword
No matter how I squint I cannot
Make out what it's pointing toward
Sometimes you feel like you've lived too long
The days drip slowly on the page
And you catch yourself
Pacing the cage

I've proved who I am so many times,
The magnetic strip's worn thin
And each time I was someone else
And everyone was taken in.
Powers chatter in high places
Stir up eddies in the dust of rage
Set me to pacing the cage.

I never knew what you all wanted
So I gave you everything.
All that I could pillage
All the spells that I could sing
It's as if the thing were written
In the constitution of the age
Sooner or later you'll wind up
Pacing the cage

Sometimes the best map will not guide you
You can't see what's round the bend.
Sometimes the road leads through dark places
Sometimes the darkness is your friend.
Today these eyes scan bleached-out land,
For the coming of the outbound stage
Pacing the cage....

—Lyrics by Bruce Cockburn—Performed by Jimmy Buffett

I'd had the chance many years earlier to grasp the message. If I'd only listened and not skipped ahead. I'd received my nod *from* "the gods".

My journey—my understanding of why I'd taken the roads I'd taken—had come full circle.

ACKNOWLEDGEMENTS

THIS MEMOIR would not have been possible without the assistance of several people.

I humbly extend my gratitude to David Hazard, an amazing writing coach, author, friend and founder of Ascent (spreadyourfire.net); my unbelievably patient and supportive wife, Pamela Ann Brunk; friend and author Bonnie Leonard and her other half, friend and social media marketing guru Matt Leonard.

I extend enormous gratitude to Jimmy Buffett, Jon Bon Jovi, the band Seether and many, many others whose music has both inspired and spoken to me on a soul level.

Lastly, my utmost gratitude to those unseen—Jibrail, the essence who inspired this memoir and constantly provides lessons in discernment and communication, Raphael, my healer compadre, teacher and fellow snark, Yeshua, the essence who continues to enlighten, provide knowing, wisdom and patience and to the teaching, nurturing spirits of wind, water, fire and earth.

JEFFREY BRUNK

is an author, artist, Lightworker and shamanic practitioner. Currently living in Northern Virginia with his wife, Pamela and two dogs, Shizzle and Shu Shu, Jeff has a Lightwork studio—Universal Touch Healing Energy—a healing sanctuary where all are welcome. He has a strong conviction that no one should be denied assistance due to financial or time constraints. "What I offer isn't about making money, it's about helping others," he says.

After several years of study and literal hands-on experience aiding people, animals and fauna using energy healing, Jeff received the Usui Reiki Master certification (though he eschews titles) through the Reiki Sanctuary of Northern Virginia. Jeff also teaches Usui Reiki and is trained in Mindfulness Meditation techniques. In addition, Jeff is an ordained non-denominational minister.

Though Jeff graduated from Randolph Technical College with a degree in Graphic Communications in 1985, his background is vast and varied. Years prior to finding his path, Jeff was a veritable jack of all trades. "When I'd gone as far as I could go or became bored with what I was doing, something new and completely different would come to me. Life is too short to spend countless days and years doing something that isn't feeding your mind, heart or soul."

Jeff has attained a Microsoft Certified Professional (MCP) certification, been a Series 6,7 and 63 licensed stockbroker for a leading brokerage firm, an art and production director for several well-known international NASCAR and baseball publications, a freelance artist, a National Sales Manager for an international blast and IED protection firm, an Eastern Regional Manager for a Japanese electronic components manufacturer, a bartender, bar manager, wine sales representative, lead paper buyer for Hearst Publishing and, lest we forget, dog walker and owner of a pet service. In other words, his resume is a pamphlet.

Jeff was born in Iowa and raised in Winston-Salem, then Lexington, North Carolina. Jeff's two children from his previous marriage are now grown. His daughter is happily married, and his son is a police officer for a major metropolitan police department. After being together four years, Jeff and Pamela wed August 29, 2011 on a beach in Key West, Florida.

www.ingramcontent.com/pod-product-compliance
Lightning Source LLC
Chambersburg PA
CBHW050537300426
44113CB00012B/2151